LETTERS

TO A

YOUNG CHRISTIAN.

BY S. J.

NEW-YORK:
AMERICAN FEMALE GUARDIAN SOCIETY.
24 BEEKMAN STREET.
1852.

Angell, Engel & Hewitt,
Printers,
1 Spruce-st., New-York.

CONTENTS.

INTRODUCTORY NOTE.

This Series of Letters recently appeared in the Advocate and Guardian under the signature of "S. J." Their perusal called forth many expressions of interest, and urgent requests that they might be re-published in a more durable form, adapted to general circulation. The Author and Publishers have acceded to these requests, hoping thus to promote the good of being.

Those who have just entered "the narrow way that leads to life," will find in this little volume *way-marks* of inestimable value, and those who are farther advanced may also gain new views of truth and duty that will prove

"A light to guide them in the road
That leads to holiness and God."

LETTERS

TO A

YOUNG CHRISTIAN.

LETTER I.

Dear Eugenia,—You are now just starting in the Christian course; you have taken the vows of God upon you, and joined yourself to his people. Henceforth you will be regarded by the world as a Christian, and they will expect you to live accordingly. They have heard you solemnly promise, that, denying all ungodliness and every worldly lust, you will live soberly, godly, and righteously, and take the Lord for your portion. Many eyes will now be upon you; and Oh, that you may be enabled to walk worthy of the profession you have made! No doubt this is your desire and purpose; perhaps a few words of counsel from one who has been longer in the way may be acceptable to you.

I have been thinking it might be well to point out some of the difficulties and dangers which the young Christian has to meet, and to unfold the nature of genuine Christian experience. I look upon those who are just entering on their religious course with a feeling almost of sadness, because they have so much to learn, and will find so much from without and from within, that may hinder their progress. It seems to me they do not generally receive from the pulpit all the specific instruction which they need. Most preachers are occupied with unfolding in a general way the doctrines and duties of religion, and attempting to awaken the impenitent. After an individual is hopefully converted, and fairly within the fold, he seems to be left to take care of himself. But at this point he needs much instruction. Many questions of conscience arise; doctrines, duties, and Christian experience present three great fields, which he has but just begun to explore. He needs a guide through each.

I can never cease to regret the time lost in the earlier part of my Christian life for want of clear ideas on these subjects. I gave myself with sincerity to the service of God, but then I had no one to tell me how much was implied in this surrender, and therefore I endeavored to ascertain by observing the course of others who had taken the same vows. This was my first great mistake. What a fruitful source of error and evil it proved to me! I long to warn every young disciple against taking the example of older professors for their guide. Yet it is so natural, that they almost invariably do it, to a greater or less extent.

Another great difficulty with me was, that I had not correct ideas of what is implied in the *life of faith.* I understood very well that heaven was not to be purchased with penances, or merited by good works. Yet the spirit of legality lingered long in my heart, unperceived. I used to think it a mark of humility for a Christian to have doubts and fears about the reality of his conversion. If I happened to hear one speak with confidence as to his good estate, I thought it savored of self-complacency, and when that Christian could say with David, "My soul shall make her boast in the Lord," it seemed to me that he was making his boast in himself.

You see that by this false view I crippled myself completely; for without Christ I could do nothing in the way of spiritual advancement, and yet, not venturing to settle the question, whether I belonged to Christ, I could not be certain that any of his offers of aid were made to *me.* The promises might be ever so large and free, yet if I was not certainly converted, what were they to me? As a consequence of this radical error, all my efforts for religious progress were made in my own strength, and of course I had only a mortifying succession of defeats. My path, instead of shining brighter and brighter unto the perfect day, grew darker and darker—strewed all along with broken resolutions. At length I lost all confidence in myself, without having gained any in God.

I thus allude to my own experience, dear Eugenia, to show why I think you, and other young Christians, may need particular instruction in regard to the inward life. I fervently desire for your own sake, and for the sake of those over whom you have an influence, and for the honor of the Master in whose service you are now enlisted, that you may avoid the mistakes into which I fell.

At another time, if the Lord permit, we will resume this subject. Meanwhile, I affectionately commend you to the care of the Good Shepherd, who carries the lambs in His bosom. Does not this convey to us a sweet impression of his tender interest in every young disciple?

Yours in the bonds of Christian love.

LETTER II.

ENTIRE CONSECRATION.

Dear Eugenia,—In a former letter I told you of some sad mistakes which I fell into in the earlier years of my Christian life. This I did, partly to explain my anxiety on your account, and partly to give you a clearer idea of your own dangers.

Do not imagine that having obtained a hope of salvation, and having made a profession of that hope before men, you have now little to do. Your parents and your pastor will be apt to have the feeling that their work for you is well nigh done, and will perhaps leave you to the sunshine and showers of Heaven. Should this be so, there will then be the more need that you should look well to yourself. There are several points which demand your earnest attention.

In the first place, you want to be *a Bible Christian.* Now do not look among the members of the church in order to find out what that is; go straight to the Bible. There you read, "Whosoever he be of you that forsaketh not all that he hath, he cannot be my disciple." *Luke* 14: 33. "If any man come to me, and hate not his father, and mother, and wife, and children, and brethren, and sisters, yea, and his own life also, he cannot be my disciple." "Thou shalt love the Lord thy God with all thy heart, and with all thy soul, and with all thy mind. This is the first and great commandment. And the second is like unto it, Thou shalt love thy neighbor as thyself." *Matt.* 22: 38—39. "Be ye therefore perfect, even as your Father in heaven is perfect." *Matt.* 5: 48. "Reckon ye also yourselves to be dead indeed unto sin, but alive unto God, through Jesus Christ our Lord." *Rom.* 6: 17.

The 12th chapter of Romans, the 13th chapter of the first book of Corinthians, and the Sermon on the Mount, give a full-length portraiture of the Bible Christian. No doubt you have read them many times, but let me ask you to read them again, as an answer to the inquiry—"What is it to be *a Bible Christian?*" You see, dear Eugenia, what you have undertaken to do—nothing less than to live up to these requirements. Those vows which you lately uttered in the house of God, in the presence of men and angels, implied all this.

Perhaps after reading these Scriptures carefully, you are ready to shrink back, and to say, "How can I undertake to come up to so high a standard? If I take these passages literally, and really go about obeying them to the letter, I shall certainly be attempting more than the church expects of me?"

You certainly will, for the standard of piety in the church now is very low, as you may easily see by comparing it with the church as it was in the days of the Apostles. She lost almost everything during the Dark Ages, and as yet has recovered herself but in part. Therefore it will never do to ask the church what you ought to be.

You see these passages and the whole spirit of the Bible demand *an entire consecration* to the Lord of all you have, and all you are, for time and eternity. This can imply nothing less than the distinct recognition at all times of the fact, that every power of your soul and body, every moment of your time, every talent and gift, all your property, all your influence, all your konwledge, and all the objects of your affection belong to God, and are to be held only as his, and for his service, with a perfect willingness on your part to relinquish any or all of them, whenever they shall be called for. It implies that you are ready to *suffer* all the will of God, and equally ready to be every moment *doing* all his will, and that you no longer allow any degree of self-will, or any form of self-seeking, and that you are actuated everywhere and at all times by the one great idea of *pleasing God.*

Perhaps you admit that this is your reasonable service, but fear to venture upon an act so solemn, lest you should not be able to live up to it. Many halt here a long time; but it is not a good place to stop. It was by an unconditional surrender that you found pardon and peace at first, and if you have not backslidden, no difficulty will be felt, except that which arises from your now having a fuller perception of what is implied in consecration, with perhaps a greater sense of your own weakness, and a stronger appreciation of the power of your spiritual enemies. It is true you are weak—very—and your enemies are strong. At the period of your conversion you could not see either of these facts as you do now; and when at that time you delighted to say and sing—

> "Relying on thy grace,
> With a glad heart and free,
> Myself, the remnant of my days,
> I consecrate to thee"—

you did not—probably could not—count the cost. You perhaps did not perceive that if you spent time, or money, or talents simply to please yourself and others, it was *robbing God;* that if you allowed any feeling of disappointment when your plans were thwarted, or felt anything different from cheerful acquiescence under painful dispensations of Providence; or allowed yourself in any little sin, or in the neglect of any duty; if you failed to listen to the suggestions of the Spirit, or hearing, failed to obey promptly and joyfully in all things; if you indulged selfishness in any form—the form of the appetites, propensities, affections, or self-will—if you allowed yourself to feel that any possession, any earthly good—health, friends, home, or anything else was essential to your happiness; if you were not willing to live in any way, and die at any time—the consecration was not *entire.*

But now you see this plainly, and therefore shrink from a distinct renewal of it. But a moment's reflection will convince you that it will not do to stop here; for how can you consistently retain the hope

Until this step is taken, nothing will be gained; take it, *and all is yours!*

"Vilest of the sinful race,
  Lo! I answer to thy call;
Meanest vessel of thy grace,
  Grace divinely free for all;
Lo! I come to do thy will,
All thy counsel to fulfil.

"If so poor a worm as I
  May to thy great glory live,
All my actions sanctify,
  All my words and thoughts receive;
Claim me for thy service, claim
All I have, and all I am.

"Take my soul and body's powers;
  Take my memory, mind, and will;
All my goods, and all my powers;
  All I know, and all I feel;
All I think, or speak, or do;
Take my heart, but make it new."

LETTER III.

GOD ACCEPTS YOU.

Dear Eugenia,—You say that entire consecration, as explained in my last letter, appears to be our reasonable service, and that nothing less is required in Scripture, but you have a painful consciousness of not living thus. Such a state of perfect devotion to God looks to you beautiful and desirable, but hopelessly out of reach.

You have then no confidence in yourself? Well, be not discouraged, but *have faith in God.* Observe in the very passage, 1 Cor. 6 : 17, 18, where he commands us to come out, and be separate, and touch not the unclean thing, he adds the precious words, "and I will receive you, and will be a Father unto you, and ye shall be my sons and daughters." You see he anticipates your difficulties, and provides for them. He knew you would feel as if you could not come up to his requirements, and so he undertakes for you. He says, "I will put my Spirit within you—I will write my law in your heart—I will lead you, and strengthen you, and uphold you—with every temptation I will make a way of escape—Lo I am with you always!"

Now may we not ask triumphantly with the apostle, "If God be for us who can be against us? Nay, in all these things we are more than conquerors through Him that loved us."

Perhaps you will ask, "May I, so young a disciple, and so unworthy, venture to think that these remarkable words can be addressed to me? Surely I must reach a higher point in the Divine life before

I can without presumption appropriate to myself these exceeding great and precious promises?"

I will reply to you, as a deeply experienced Christian once did to me, when I made the same objection. "So you think that after you have done a few more things for God he will begin to love you?"

This answer struck me forcibly. I saw at once the spirit of *legality* which I had unconsciously been cherishing. From that moment I began to embrace those promises, which before I had only seen afar off. I had been many years a church member, but had made no progress in the divine life; how could I and how can any one, while from obstinacy, or timidity, or unbelief, they decline the offered aid of heaven? I stood trembling before the requirements of God, exclaiming with the Psalmist, "Thy commandment is exceeding broad," but I did not then perceive that the promise was as broad as the command.

The Saviour says that all he requires of us is comprised in two commandments; the first is, "Thou shalt love the Lord thy God with all thy heart." Now, you love the Lord, but not as yet with all your heart, for you still find something of selfishness remaining. You ask, "How am I to meet this requirement—how shall I ever be rid of all self-seeking and self-will?"

Your gracious God knew that after having lived to yourself so many years, it would seem to you an utter impossibility to bring the principle of self-love back into its right place, and foreseeing the perplexity with which you would look at this first and great command, he meets you with a *promise* couched in the very words of the precept, "The Lord thy God will circumcise thine heart, and the heart of thy seed, to love the Lord thy God with all thine heart, and with all thy soul, that thou mayest live," Deut. 30 : 6. That which you feel yourself unable to do, he offers to do for you.

"These," you say, "are comfortable words, but on what condition will he do such great things for me?"

The first condition is, that you heartily *desire* it. It must be an earnest all-absorbing desire. You must feel as David did when he said, "As the hart panteth after the water brooks, so panteth my soul after thee, O God." "Blessed are they that hunger and thirst after righteousness, for they shall be filled." But desire alone, however ardent, never makes the promises available. If you get no further than desire, you will sigh and go backward. Alas, alas, it is just here that multitudes of the church get, and no farther! They wish they were holy—they wish they had more faith—they wish they were not so selfish—but year after year passes, and nothing is gained. They would give up their hope altogether, only they think so many good desires must have a gracious origin—that they should not love good things, and have from time to time these devout aspirations, if a work of grace was not begun in their souls. This is a fatal mistake. Desires which are not strong enough to move the will furnish no evidence in their favor.

2. To this fervent desire must be added *faith.* That is, you must believe the promises, and realise that they are addressed to you. You must accept them, rest on them, and never let go of them. These two things, *desire* and *faith,* in connection with the *entire consecration* described in my last letter, form the conditions on which all the great and precious promises become yours.

Perhaps at this point of your experience you will feel a difficulty, which many others have felt. You have given yourself to the Lord, and you desire above all things to love him with your whole heart, and you see here an offer on his part to come and meet you, as the father did his prodigal son, and afford the needful assistance, but you dare not accept it just now—you are waiting to have some remarkable feelings. I remember that I halted here a long time, but at length, I was obliged to believe that God would help me, not on account of anything particularly marked in my religious feelings, but simply *because he had said he would.*

Yes, dear Eugenia, you may be sure of this, that so long as you live for God, and cherish an intense desire to love Him with all your heart, there is—there can be—nō presumption in believing that the promises are yours. Calculate as largely as you may on his aid, he will not be displeased; raise your expectations ever so high, He will never disappoint them; for He "is able to do exceeding abundantly above all that we ask or think, according to the power that worketh in us." Eph. 3 : 20.

Yours in the bonds of Christian love.

"Lord, give me faith! He hears—what grace is this?
Dry up thy tears, my soul, and cease to grieve!
He shows me what he did, and who he is,—
I must, I will, I can, *I do believe.*"

LETTER IV.

ENTERING ON THE LIFE OF FAITH.

Dear Eugenia,—Having as I trust given yourself without reserve to the Lord, in the full belief that he accepts you (not on account of any remarkable feelings, but because *he has said he would*), and having taken the next step, that of throwing yourself on his promises, you may feel that the foundation of Christian experience is laid—a broad and beautiful foundation, Jesus Christ himself being the Chief Corner Stone.

You have made a good beginning, but you would not stop here? The object of laying a foundation is, that we may build upon it. You are happy in the service of your new Master. The determination to please Him gives you pleasure. His yoke is easy now, because it is fairly put on; his burden is light, for he lets you lay it on him. You are never weary of saying

"I am my Lord's, and He is mine."

Yes, "Wisdom's ways are ways of pleasantness, and all her paths are peace." You feel that all is on the altar; but perhaps after a while, when you have learned to take broader views of duty, and have become more discriminating in regard to religious experience, you will make some unwelcome discoveries. You may find that you have been unconsciously allowing some form of selfishness. In such a case, I have two words of counsel to offer. Some Christians are unwilling to see anything of this kind, when the faithful monitor within would fain draw their attention to it, because they do not like to think they have made any mistake in the matter of consecration. There are others, who when they find anything wrong in their feelings or practice, seem surprised and disheartened; their zeal is damped, their faith fails, and if they do not say it in so many words, they have a feeling like this; "I thought the Lord was going to keep me, and he has not."

Now my two words of counsel are, *first*, Don't be unwilling to see the worst of yourself; *second*, Don't be discouraged at the sight. As soon as you discover any infirmity, defect, bad habit, any form of selfishness, or anything that hinders you in the Divine life, carry it at once to the Lord Jesus Christ, and ask Him to take it away. Remember that he has offered to "supply all your need," "purge away all your dross," and "sanctify you wholly." If you are honest, he is faithful, and all will be well.

Never for one moment give way to *discouragement.* "All discouragement is of the nature of unbelief." Unbelief is fatal to every grace. Nothing seems to grieve the Spirit so much. The best thing you can do, is, to be all the time trying to strengthen your faith. To this end, make the PROMISES your *study.* Have them all in your memory and in your heart. Keep them bright by constant use. Dwell much on the assurances of God's love, with which the Scriptures abound. Endeavor to get a full, deep persuasion of His love to you, and let your heart triumph in the wonderful fact. Do not let the adversary rob you of this belief, that He loves you with a tenderness unutterable—a love far, far beyond that of any earthly friend. Does this seem too much? Look at the proofs of it in what He is doing for you every moment, in what He has been doing for you ever since your birth, and in what He did for you ages before, when every one of your wants was anticipated, and provided for—when every one of your sins was anticipated, and atoned for. Dwell on these things, and then read those sweet words, "*I have loved thee with an everlasting love.*"

I dwell on this subject the more, because I find in my own experience there is nothing like being fully persuaded that God loves me. Realising this, I cannot help loving Him, and thus all duties are made easy, and all trials light. In this state of mind there is no difficulty in appropriating the promises; indeed after a while you will hardly need to draw upon them, for you will realise so fully and sweetly that *the Promiser himself is yours.* They will then be to you as "the kisses of his mouth."—Cant. 1: 2.

But while I speak of the happiness which is found in loving God, and believing that he loves you, I ought to throw in a caution against making your own enjoyment an ultimate end. There is such a thing as seeking more religion for the sake of a higher happiness, and aspiring after holiness, that we may take complacency in it, and desiring God's spiritual gifts, rather than himself. These are hidden forms of selfishness, which escape notice for a long time. Frequently God is compelled to withdraw from his children the light of his countenance for a while, in order to bring these evils to light.

If at any time your feelings should not be so lively as they now are, be not discouraged. Remember the feelings of God do not change with yours. Remember, too, that religion does not consist in joy. The abiding peace promised to the believer, depends not upon joy, but upon faith. God sometimes tries his children, to see if they will follow him in the dark. Lean on the arm of your Beloved, when called to walk in the "night of faith." The question is not "How have you felt to-day? Have you enjoyed your mind?" But "*For whom are you living? Is all on the altar?*"

"Man shall not live by bread alone, but by every word that proceedeth out of the mouth of God." "The just shall live by faith." Not by joys, not by tender emotions, not by vivid perceptions of truth, not by dreams, visions, and manifestations—these may be all good and desirable, but they are special indulgences—they are not the things to *live on.* Full faith in every word which proceedeth out of the mouth of God, is that alone which makes a strong, happy, useful Christian.

That you, my dear Eugenia, may be a Christian of this stamp, is the fervent prayer of your affectionate friend.

LETTER V.

THE HOLY SPIRIT.

"The blest Redeemer, ere He breathed
His tender, last farewell,
A Guide, a Comforter, bequeathed,
With us to dwell."

"And every virtue we possess,
And every victory won,
And every thought of holiness
Are His alone."

Dear Eugenia,—Having now made some trial of the life of faith, you find it a good way, an easy way, a safe way. So far as you trust in God, he meets your faith, and you think if you trusted him perfectly, he would meet every want of the soul entirely. No doubt this is true.

"Venture on Him—venture wholly—
Let no other trust intrude."

There is a world of wisdom in the exhortation of Paul: "As ye have, therefore, received Christ Jesus the Lord, so walk ye in Him." You entered on the divine life by an act of faith and consecration; nothing but continual faith and consecration can carry you forward.

To this end it is important that you should form

the habit of *inward recollection.* By this I mean, that you are ever to bear in mind "Whose you are, and whom you serve." While your thoughts are necessarily occupied about other things, let there be a leaning of the heart on Christ—an attitude of the affections, which says continually, "Hold thou me up and I shall be safe." You complain that you sometimes forget to lean on him, and remark that you need to have a prompter ever at hand, to remind you of your duty. You do indeed need such a prompter, and so does every Christian, young or old. Our blessed Saviour knew it would be so, and graciously provided for this want.

Shortly before he left his disciples, he told them, that sadly as they felt about his leaving them, they would be gainers by it, for the third person in the Trinity would come to take his place, and abide with them forever! He then proceeded to tell them what this wonderful Guest would do; that he would guide them into all truth, and bring to remembrance those instructions of his which they had forgotten, or had not understood; that he would be a Comforter, and direct them at all times what to do and what to say.

I suppose the disciples gazed at their Lord with a perplexed and troubled expression, for they did not understand him. They were so much afflicted at the idea of his leaving them, that they probably felt it impossible for any one else to supply his place.

the habit of *inward recollection.* By this I mean, that you are ever to bear in mind "Whose you are, and whom you serve." While your thoughts are necessarily occupied about other things, let there be a leaning of the heart on Christ—an attitude of the affections, which says continually, "Hold thou me up and I shall be safe." You complain that you sometimes forget to lean on him, and remark that you need to have a prompter ever at hand, to remind you of your duty. You do indeed need such a prompter, and so does every Christian, young or old. Our blessed Saviour knew it would be so, and graciously provided for this want.

Shortly before he left his disciples, he told them, that sadly as they felt about his leaving them, they would be gainers by it, for the third person in the Trinity would come to take his place, and abide with them forever! He then proceeded to tell them what this wonderful Guest would do; that he would guide them into all truth, and bring to remembrance those instructions of his which they had forgotten, or had not understood; that he would be a Comforter, and direct them at all times what to do and what to say.

I suppose the disciples gazed at their Lord with a perplexed and troubled expression, for they did not understand him. They were so much afflicted at the idea of his leaving them, that they probably felt it impossible for any one else to supply his place.

Afterwards they understood it, and often spoke of themselves and their conv[illegible] as "Temples of the Holy Ghost." This appears to me a remarkable expression. "Will God indeed dwell on the earth?" Such he assures us is the fact, and certainly from a fact so wonderful and glorious, Christians ought to derive more comfort and strength than they generally do. Here is the Guide, the prompter, the ever-present, ever-watchful friend, which you feel that you so much need.

Do you ask, "On what conditions can I have this friend always with me?"

You recollect that in a former letter I stated the conditions on which the great and precious promises of God would be fulfilled to you; now the promise of the indwelling of the Spirit is the greatest and most precious of them all. The Saviour speaks of it as "*The Promise* of the Father"—something above and beyond all others—that which constitutes the distinguishing characteristic of the Gospel dispensation. The conditions here are the same as in regard to the other promises; viz.: *desire* and *faith*. If you really wish to have the constant presence of such a glorious Guest, be assured he is ready to come and take up his abode with you.

This willingness he has strongly expressed in many passages of Scripture, particularly that interesting one in Revelation 3 : 20, where he represents himself as standing at the door of the heart, and knocking for admittance; also in that sweet assurance, Luke 11: 13, "If ye, then, being evil, know how to give good gifts unto your children, how much more shall your Heavenly Father give the Holy Spirit to them that ask Him?" Throw yourself continually on this assurance, and as God is true, you shall continually have the presence of the Comforter.

In addition to this desire for his presence, and this belief in it, you must form a habit of listening for his suggestions, and rendering a prompt obedience. Do not ask him to guide you, if you intend to guide yourself. Do not ask him to sanctify you, unless you are willing to renounce all sin. Do not ask him to make clear the path of duty, if you are not intending to walk in it. Do not ask him to work in you to will and to do of his good pleasure, unless you are ready to co-operate with him. Do not ask him to make a way of escape for you in every temptation, unless you really mean to escape. Do not ask him to comfort and sustain you under trials, and then refuse to accept of his consolations. Do not ask him to be with you all the day, and then immediately break away from him. O how constantly is the Holy Spirit mocked and grieved by such prayers!

On the other hand if you desire and determine to *live as you pray*, you will find him at all times ready to help. Are you going into company? Ask the Spirit to take charge of your conversation. Are you called to the house of mourning? Ask him to give you appropriate feelings, and teach you how to administer consolation to the afflicted. Are you called to suffering and trial? Do not grieve the Spirit by refusing to accept the comfort he offers Have you difficult duties to discharge?—duties requiring more wisdom than you seem to possess? Here is that gracious Friend, who has said, "If any man lack wisdom let him ask of God, who giveth to all men liberally and upbraideth not, and it shall be given him. But let him ask in faith, nothing wavering." Never forget his presence. You cannot afford to lose the comfort of it—you cannot safely lose the restraint of it.

It should be remembered also, not only that God *offers* us this aid, but he *commands* us to accept it. "Be filled with the Spirit," is a command as binding upon us as any one in the decalogue—is it not? Have you ever thought seriously of trying to obey this command? The primitive Christians obeyed it —why should not we? You must never rest satisfied until you are *filled with the Spirit.* Perhaps you will here ask the same question which I once put to an experienced Christian: "How shall I know when I am filled with the Spirit?" The reply was, "When you bring forth all the fruits of the Spirit (love, joy, peace, long-suffering, faith, meekness, temperance), on their appropriate occasions." It does not necessarily imply ecstatic joy, or high emotions of any kind, but a soul in such a well-balanced state, that the Saviour can manifest himself through it appropriately on all occasions.

If you are wholly the Lord's, you will attempt obedience to every requirement. His own gentle words are, "If ye love, me keep my commandments." Now, therefore, be not disobedient to this most gracious, most important command, "BE FILLED WITH THE SPIRIT." It is found in Eph. 5 : 18. The three succeeding verses show how a person will live who is thus filled.

The grace of the Lord Jesus Christ, and the love of God, and *the communion of the Holy Ghost*, be with you ALWAYS.

LETTER VI.

CRUCIFIXION OF THE DESIRES.

Dear Eugenia,—You inquire what is meant by that passage in Galatians, "They that are Christ's have crucified the flesh with the affections and lusts." I am glad your attention has been turned to this subject, for it is a very important one. Many

Christians, for want of clear ideas in regard to the nature and extent of that self-crucifixion required in this and similar Scriptures, go on for years without making any real progress in the Divine life. They are sinfully self-indulgent without being fully aware of it. They experience a feeling of condemnation, are conscious something is wrong, but do not know precisely what it is. They have been told in general terms that they must deny themselves and take up their cross, but when or where, they do not exactly see.

The great Creator has endowed us all with certain desires; viz.: the appetites, propensities and affections. It is the nature of these desires to demand gratification, therefore there is nothing wrong in gratifying them up to a certain point; that point is, *the attainment of the objects for which they were implanted.* But as their gratification is attended with pleasure, we, in our inordinate self-love, are prone to indulge them beyond that point; it then becomes sinful.

You know very well what the *appetites* and *affections* are; the *propensities* are more numerous and varied in their characteristics. Some of the principal ones are curiosity, or the desire of knowledge; acquisitiveness, or the desire of possession; self-love, or the desire of happiness; sociality, or the desire of society; desire of power, desire of esteem, and imitativeness. Inasmuch as these are original desires, forming a part of our constitution, they are all innocent, and not only innocent, but useful. Therefore, when the Apostle speaks of crucifying them, he does not mean to annihilate, but only to put a stop to their inordinate activity. The first step towards this is to ascertain precisely what is the *healthy action* in each case.

1. In regard to the *Appetites*, the most prominent of which is the desire for food, drink, and sleep; it is evident that they should not be indulged for the sake of the gratification they afford, but simply to meet the wants of the body. This rule commends itself to the reason of every one, yet many plausible excuses are invented for evading it. It is by no means easy to break up long habits of self-indulgence in these respects. But it must be done, or the flesh will war against the Spirit and bring it into captivity, and keep it in captivity; it must be done, otherwise there will be little or no progress in the divine life.

2d. In regard to the *Propensities.* When we give ourselves to the Lord, we lay them all upon the altar. They are not to be extinguished, but completely subordinated. We cannot rush heedlessly forward in the gratification of any one of them, as we may heretofore have done; and for this simple reason our own pleasure is never more to be the ultimate end in anything we do, great or small; our business is to please God.

For instance, you have the propensity of *curiosity*, or the desire of knowledge. You think this is very good, and a thing to be cherished; so it is—but with restrictions. You are not at liberty now to press eagerly forward in pursuit of knowledge, as perhaps you used to do, simply for the pleasure of the pursuit, or the advantages of its attainment. You can now seek only the kind and degree of knowledge which God permits, and that only to glorify Him. So in regard to the other propensities. They all have an instinctive and a voluntary action. So far as they are instinctive, they are without any moral character. Their voluntary action is good or bad according as they are used for God or self.

3d. In regard to the *Affections*. Here, too, there must be something done in the way of regulation and subordination. The Saviour expresses it very strongly when he says, "If any man come to me, and hate not his father, and mother, and wife, and children, and brethren, and sisters, he cannot be my disciple." Luke 14 : 26. That is, these natural affections, however amiable in themselves, must be so completely subordinated to the love of God, that when the question is between pleasing our friends and pleasing him, we shall go contrary to their wishes, and thus act as if we hated them. It implies, moreover, that we love God so much better than earthly friends as to be willing to give them all up whenever he shall call for them.

All this I suppose to be implied in the words of the Apostle, "They that are Christ's have crucified the flesh with the affections and lusts." You will find multitudes of professors who evidently know nothing of this crucifixion; but Paul would say, "They are not Christ's."

Does it seem to you, my dear young friend, a great thing thus to have every thought brought into captivity to the obedience of Christ? It *is* a great thing. It can never be done in your own unaided strength. But it is no matter how hard any work is, provided only you have help enough. If you call to mind what I said in my last letter, you will see that great as the work is, *you have help enough.* Only avail yourself of that help, and your triumphant song will be, "Through Christ strengthening me, I can do all things!" However clamorous any appetite or propensity may be, and however it may have been strengthened by long indulgence, if you are determined that henceforth it shall keep its place, and *at the moment of temptation*, throw yourself in simple, full-hearted faith on the promised aid of the indwelling Spirit, will that aid, think you, be wanting? "God is faithful, who will not suffer you to be tempted above that ye are able, but will with the temptation also make a way to escape." 1 *Cor.* 10 : 13. "In all things we are more than conquerors, through Him that loved us." *Rom.* 8 : 37.

Perhaps you cast your eyes around amongst your Christian friends, and can scarcely find any who seem to be thus victorious. This disheartens you. I remember well how depressing it was to me. In spite of the commands and encouragements of Scripture, I felt as if it would savor of presumption in me to expect success where so many had failed. But now I see clearly, and feel deeply, how wrong it was to be drawing discouragement from the example of others, instead of drawing strength from the promises of God. I was commanded to be looking unto Jesus —instead of that, I kept looking at my poor fellowmen.

If you have not as yet met with any case where grace appeared to be completely triumphant, do not too hastily conclude that there are no such cases. There is abundant evidence that in all ages, and perhaps in all churches, there have been instances of this kind. It is my happiness to know a considerable number, who can testify that they find (and have for years,) that the grace of God is sufficient for them at all times, and under all circumstances—that in every temptation he makes a way of escape for them—that he keeps them in *perfect peace*—and they have always a blessed consciousness that the

Holy Spirit dwells in them, and is continually holding them back from the indulgence of wrong feelings. This is their own testimony; they feel it to be so, and everything in their lives goes to show that it is so. The strongest desire of my heart is, that all the dear children of God may reach forth the hand of faith and *take* what he is so ready to *give.* If they will meet him by *consecration*, *faith*, and *the crucifixion of all inordinate desires*, he on his part will not fail to meet them with all the blessings of his grace. Then will they be truly happy, and then they will be in that attitude where God can use them to his own glory, and to their satisfaction.

" Die daily; from the touch of sin recede,—
Then thou hast crowned Him, and He reigns indeed."

LETTER VII.

PRAYER.

Dear Eugenia,—You ask my views on the subject of *Prayer.* I hardly feel willing to enter on this topic, for it has so many bearings and relations, that the limits of a letter cannot do it justice.

Much has been said and written about prayer; yet no one understands it till taught by the Spirit. I have reason to think there is a great deal of concealed scepticism on this subject—a scepticism so far concealed as to be hidden in a considerable degree from those who are the subjects of it. They doubt the efficacy of prayer; at least, of their own prayers. If they should look into their hearts, they would see the reason; they are acting a double part—asking for spiritual blessings which they do not really desire. No wonder such prayers are unheeded—no wonder they have so little confidence in them.

Satan will be likely to assail you sometimes with temptations in regard to prayer. At first he will try to make you think that such poor prayers as yours can never reach the ear of God. Tell him that, poor as they are, you have an Advocate with the Father, who has promised to present them. Here perhaps he will suggest that your petitions are so badly interlined with wandering thoughts, that they are not fit to be presented at the court of Heaven, and even the Great Intercessor himself will be ashamed to offer them! Tell him God forgives the wanderings of the intellect, when he knows the heart is fixed.

At other times the tempter may insinuate very plausibly, that as the Almighty has laid his plan, it will assuredly be carried out, and therefore there is no use in prayer. Tell him we might think so too, had not God himself assured us to the contrary. True, his plans are all laid—not one jot or tittle of them will fail; his *instrumentalities* too are all chosen, and the prayers of the saints form an important part of these instrumentalities. Could anything be more kind and condescending than that the Great Ruler of the universe should allow his subjects to come to him about so many things? He permits them to pray for all men; for kings and all that are in authority, for the sick and afflicted, for the church and the ministry, for those who love, and for those who hate them, for the conversion of sinners, and the sanctification of saints, and even for all their own little wants, temporal as well as spiritual. Here is your permit—" In *everything* by prayer and supplication, with thanksgiving, let your requests be made known unto God." How pleasant it is for young Christians to have so many errands to the Throne of Grace—so many excuses for seeking an interview with God—so many topics on which they may converse with him!

It must be confessed that at first sight, prayer seems a strange instrumentality to be used in the accomplishment of the designs of God. But we see in it *our Father's heart.* He knew that anything which should bring us into his presence would do us good—make us better and happier. He tells us in his holy word that we must pray—that prayer is the medium through which he conveys his favors. " Ask and receive, that your joy may be full."

The adversary will perhaps assail you on another

point. He will suggest that there are multitudes of prayers, put up by good people every day, that do not seem to be answered. This objection you can meet in several ways. In the first place, "Delay is not denial." Many of these petitions are already answered in the heart of God, but the answer is not made apparent. "The Lord is a God of judgment, blessed are all they that *wait* for him." Yes, it is a blessed thing to learn to *wait*. In the next place, many of these prayers are not offered in faith, and "Whatsoever is not of faith is sin." Then, too, many prayers are not offered with entire submission to the Divine will. They are selfish, and God cannot be expected to answer them. Then again, petitions offered by persons who are living in any allowed sin, of omission or commission, in thought, word, or deed, have no claim on the promises to prayer. The Psalmist says, "If I regard iniquity in my heart, the Lord will not hear me."

Here perhaps the adversary will take another turn and say, "Then nobody's prayers are heard, for no one is without some iniquity in his heart." But the Psalmist says in another place, "Verily God hath heard *me*." If David, under the old dispensation, came into that state of purity that his prayers could be heard, then surely you, under the brighter light of the new, may come there.

Is your confidence in the efficacy of prayer

weakened by seeing so many petitions go unanswered? Be assured that it is owing to the want of consecration or faith on the part of the petitioners. For as God is true, all prayer offered by the soul that is wholly given up, and in the exercise of full faith, is answered. Indeed it must be so, even if no promise had been made to prayer, for such a soul, being in sympathy with God, desires only what God desires; it must be so, for the Holy Spirit inspires the petition; it must be so, for

"Prayer is appointed to convey
The blessings God designs to give."

Do not ask for anything but what you want. How often have I, in the prayer of the morning, asked the Lord to guide me through the day. But I knew not what I asked. I had no idea of being momentarily under Divine direction, and each day showed that I preferred to guide myself. I used to ask Him to keep me from sin, while at the same time there were several forms of sin which I was not willing to give up. I used to ask Him to humble me; yet if anything occurred which was calculated to do this, the vexation and mortification which I allowed myself to feel abundantly proved that I had been asking for something I did not want.

When you have asked for what you really want, *wait* for the answer; expect it; calculate upon it;

and be willing to have it come in a different form from what you had anticipated. Of course if you pray aright you always express a paramount wish that the will of the Lord may be done; to be consistent, then, you must be satisfied to have your prayer answered by having that will done. One thing is certain, "God never denies his children anything, but with the design of giving them something better."

Do not allow your prayers to be always in the form of *petitions*. Let thanksgiving, praise, and expressions of affectionate confidence abound in them. You have a beautiful example in the book of Psalms, and you would do well to study it, as a model of devotional exercises. How often does the Psalmist begin with a lament, and end with a shout!

It is only the child who loves his Father, and is conscious that the great aim of his life is to please Him, who knows what it is to "draw near with a true heart in full assurance of faith." For him there is a standing invitation to "come boldly unto the Throne of Grace, that he may obtain mercy, and find grace to help in time of need." If you live right, you will pray right. If you keep everything on the altar, and are in the constant exercise of faith, you will, as you advance, come into all the mysteries of prayer. You will learn from your own blessed experience what is meant by "the prayer of faith," and what it is to have the Spirit helping your infirmities; what it is to "pray without ceasing," and to obtain all you ask; and what it is to have the soul "rest in the single petition, 'Thy will be done,' as in its pleasant and perpetual home!"

LETTER VIII.

BE A BIBLE CHRISTIAN.

Dear Eugenia,—You say that the command of Scripture is, "Come out from *the world*, and be separate," but that I seem to be requiring you to come out from the *church*. It is true the standard of Christian attainment I would hold up to you is far above that which is usually seen among professors of religion in the present day. But you and I are not Roman Catholics, and do not believe in the infallibility of the church. We cannot feel bound by her creed or her practice, for both have varied much in different ages. Alas, how widely have we departed from the spirit and practice, if not from the principles of the primitive church! Whatever might have been true among the early Christians, it certainly is not safe now for young converts to take the good people around them for their example. Even in those days of comparative purity, Paul cautioned them against measuring themselves by themselves, and comparing themselves among themselves, and said that such were not wise.

When a young Christian first comes into the church, he is apt to look round and observe how the members live,—how far, and in what things, they conform to the world, what duties are considered important, and how many it will answer to omit. From this survey he forms a judgment as to how much is expected of him, and if he succeed in meeting these expectations, he is very apt to think he has done enough. He may not do all this deliberately, but he naturally and imperceptibly falls in with the current. Without you are specially on your guard, and have the special grace of God, your feet will slide just here. Your pastor tells you not to take older Christians for your guide; but unless you have uncommon decision of character you will scarcely rise above so strong an influence.

It appears to me that of all the dangers which beset the path of the young pilgrim this is the greatest! With shame and sorrow I must say to you, that church members now are generally so far below the Bible standard and the primitive model, that the young convert in putting himself under their watch and care gains but little, and often loses the high aspirations and good resolutions with which he sets out.

The command is, "Be not conformed to the world;" neither must you be conformed to the church, when she has become like the world. Do not suffer yourself to be deceived by names: the true church consists of those only who are truly living for God; the rest must be ranked with the world, whatever profession they may make. Of course, then, there is no propriety in our allowing them to influence us. Now without being uncharitable, or pretending to judge in doubtful cases as to whether such and such persons have ever been converted, we cannot help seeing whether they are really living for God; and where it is apparent they are not, why we must come out from among them and be separate, just as much as we would from the rest of the world. He that is to give account for himself should think for himself. Do not, my dear Eugenia, allow others to think for you—they cannot stand for you at the bar of judgment. Remember you have only one life to live, and if you make any mistakes you cannot come back to rectify them.

Oh, if each young convert would take the Bible for his guide, resolving in the strength of the Lord to be a *Bible Christian*, without any regard whatever to the opinions and practices of others, in the church or out of it, what a gainer he would be! How much the cause of Christ would gain, how much would God be honored! Then would Zion arise from the dust and put on her beautiful garments.

Now let us look into the Bible and see what it requires. And first, we are met by this command, "Whether therefore ye eat or drink, or whatsoever ye do, do all to the glory of God." That is, do nothing to please yourself, or to please others, but in everything, from the greatest to the smallest, seek to please and honor God. Do you not see that this one precept cuts you off entirely from doing things merely because others do? To your own Master you stand or fall.

But you say it is very hard for a young Christian to take such a decided stand—it seems like setting yourself up to be better and wiser than those who have been in the church a long time before you.

I know it is hard—very—but it must be done, if you would keep a conscience void of offence. If you are commanded to *hate* father and mother, the presumption is, that you are not to care a great deal for anybody else—of course I mean where they come in the way of duty.

Now we will take another look into the Bible. The next passage that meets us is this: "To him that esteemeth anything to be unclean, to him it is unclean!" Romans 14: 14. Here again you see it won't do to go by other people's ideas of right and wrong. Suppose you are a babe in Christ, and the rest of the church are far advanced, still, if certain things in which they allow themselves seem wrong to you, according to this passage, they would be wrong for you. Though you cannot always judge for others, you can and must always judge for yourself.

Take another passage of Scripture: "Whatsoever is not of faith is sin;" and another, "Let every one be fully persuaded in his own mind." That is, never do anything which you do not fully believe to be according to the mind of God. The Holy Spirit offers to guide you *in all things;* if you are right, you have put yourself under His guidance, and now if you do anything which you are not satisfied He calls you to do, that thing is not done in faith—it is sin. The moment you begin to follow others, *that moment you desert your Guide.*

My dear young friend, you cannot be too much on your guard against surrounding influences. If you would be a consistent, happy Christian, if you would please God, if you would make any progress in the Divine life, if you would make your influence felt on the church and the world, you must think for yourself, read the Bible for yourself, judge for yourself as to its requisitions, and ACT UP FULLY TO YOUR OWN CONVICTIONS OF DUTY.

LETTER IX.

CHOOSING ASSOCIATES.

Dear Eugenia,—Having settled upon the principles which should regulate your life, we will now proceed to make some application of them. It is one thing to *receive* the truths of the Gospel, and quite another to *apply* them.

The first subject which naturally comes up, is *the choice of associates.* This is a matter of very great importance. We are so constituted that we cannot be insensible to the pleasures of society and friendship; they seem essential to our happiness and wellbeing. You have perhaps hitherto mingled freely in society, and chosen for your intimates those nearest you in age, and similar in respect to education, taste, and sympathies, without taking into consideration particularly their influence on you, or yours on them. But you are now in a new position; having devoted yourself to the Lord, you cannot choose your friends and associates without His permission. In all your social intercourse now, you have two objects in view: viz., to do good, or to get good. You will not talk for the sake of talking, or allow the conversation to flow on without aim or benefit, for you feel that your Lord's time must not be wasted;

moreover, I trust the love of Christ constraineth you to have your conversation always as becometh saints.

Therefore, while you associate with those who feel differently, for the sake of doing them good, you will choose for your intimate friends, not persons who are most pleasing in a worldly point of view, but those who have most of the spirit of Christ. This you will do in the first place, because, if your heart is right, it will flow out towards such most warmly and tenderly; and second, because you will feel that the Saviour approves this choice; and third, because they will be a great help to you in the Divine life.

Although it is natural for you to prefer the company of those of your own age, it would be greatly for your advantage to associate as much as possible with older Christians. You may profit much by their experience. I have known some friendships between the old and the young, that were mutually delightful, and to the younger parties eminently advantageous. Perhaps you feel as if one farther advanced than yourself could not wish for a friendship where the benefit was likely to be all on one side. "Remember the words of the Lord Jesus, how he said, 'it is more blessed to give than to receive.'" Thus, if the younger is to be the gainer in one way, the elder is in another. Hitherto you have not, perhaps, felt disposed to associate much with those who lacked education, refinement, and all that goes to constitute your idea of the agreeable. Some of the Lord's disciples are quite deficient in these respects, yet He loves them, and you, if in sympathy with Him, will love them too, and choose their company and their friendship in preference to those who are more refined, but less spiritual.

These humble disciples, who have not had the advantages of education and intercourse with cultivated society, you will find, not unfrequently, have been taught of the Spirit in a remarkable degree, and can teach you much on the great subject of Christian experience. Others may tell you what they have read, but these can tell you what they feel and know. Such individuals have always been to me the most powerful of preachers. I have been more interested and enlightened, more encouraged and animated, by listening to the religious experience of some humble disciple, than by the most eloquent discourses.

I know that the matter of associates is not altogether under your own control; you are often obliged to be on familiar, if not intimate terms, with those whose society is not particularly interesting or profitable. They may be family connections, or near neighbors, or in some way have a claim on you. In these cases you must be patient, regarding it as an arrangement of Providence; and remember, in all your intercourse with them, that either you will do them good, or they will do you hurt.

It is not best to have many intimate friends, lest it should take up too much of your time. Pleasant and profitable as your intercourse may be, it should not be suffered to trench on other things which demand attention. When called to go into company, or to receive friends, remember whose you are, and whom you serve, and be always intent on your great work. Lift up your heart to God for his presence and blessing, and ask him to take charge of the conversation. Always converse as you would if the Lord Jesus Christ were present to your bodily eye, as He ever is to the eye of faith.

May you be divinely guided, my dear Eugenia, in this most important matter of choosing friends and associates. Much of your happiness and well-being depend upon it. It is an old saying, "A man is known by the company he keeps," and we might almost add, a young person is *made* by the company he keeps. You will insensibly imbibe the feelings and views of those with whom you associate. If you were willing to be a worldly-minded professor, rather gay and fashionable, you might choose associates of that stamp; for, alas, there are plenty of them. But if you mean to be a whole-souled Christian, and have it the one great *object*, and the one great *rule* of life *to please God*, then choose persons of this stamp for your friends. "Iron sharpeneth iron."

Yours in the sweet bonds of the Gospel.

LETTER X.

MARRIAGE.

"How blest the sacred tie that binds
In union sweet, according minds!
How swift the heavenly course they run,
Whose hearts, and faith, and hopes are one!"

Dear Eugenia,—In my last I considered the subject of *Associates* in general. This naturally leads to the consideration of the principles which should guide young Christians in the choice of *a companion for life*. If it behoves them to be careful in the selection of their ordinary associates, how much more in regard to entering into a relation so intimate and permanent as that of marriage! This is the last subject that should be treated with levity, for no movement in life is fraught with more serious consequences. The truly consecrated cannot speak lightly of it, but will feel that here, as in everything else, all must be referred to God. The Divine guidance will be sought with an honest intention of following it. But, alas, how many there are who ask the Lord to direct them, and yet after all intend to follow their own inclinations!

In my last letter I was led to remark, that having devoted yourself to the Lord, you could not choose your friends and associates without his permission. If this be true of ordinary friends and associates, how much more in regard to choosing a companion for life! You are not your own. This fact fully realised leaves no room for independent action. That Master, whose you are and whom you serve, must dictate every movement. The one great idea ever before your mind is to please Him. While you need not and ought not to enter into a relation so intimate and endearing with one who is not agreeable to you, and able to command your warmest affections, still this must not be the primary consideration. You may and must consult your own taste, and your own heart, but not till you have first inquired and satisfied yourself that you have the approval of your Heavenly Father. The requirement of Scripture is that we marry "*only in the Lord.*"

Now, if you should suffer yourself to follow the dictates of fancy or feeling, without honestly seeking to know the will of God in the matter, however worthy the object of your affections might be, you could not be said to "marry in the Lord." There are many professed disciples of Christ who, while they acknowledge their obligations to do everything else to the glory of God, seem to think that in this thing they may please themselves. I do not know by what authority they take this most important matter out from under His jurisdiction. If ever a young person needs heavenly wisdom and divine guidance, it is here, where there is so much at stake, and such a liability to be misled by fancy and feeling. Let us thank the Lord, then, that He will permit us to consult Him.

If the ruling desire of your heart is to please God, you will not allow your affections to be placed on one who does not sympathise in this desire. For how can two walk together except they be agreed? If the grand motive of action be with you one thing, and with him another, you cannot expect to move on comfortably together. Besides, with a heart full of love to God, you will not enjoy the society of one who is a stranger to that love. The subjects nearest your heart have no interest for him. I do not see how you can ever form an attachment to a man of the world until you have first become yourself a backslider. Should you find your affections taking such a direction, it would be high time to inquire if you had not lost your first love.

Not long since I put this question to the members of my Bible Class: "Is it right for a Christian to marry an impenitent person?" The question went round the class, and each one said that it did not seem to be right, yet no one was prepared to pronounce it absolutely wrong. I then asked them if they could bring any argument in its favor. They could think of only one, and that was, the possibility that it might result in the conversion of the impenitent partner. I admitted that this was sometimes the case, but reminded them *how much oftener* the influence went the other way.

To marry a man with the hope of converting him is a most dangerous experiment. The strong probability is, that he will gradually undermine your piety, draw you more and more into conformity with the world, and nullify your influence in your family. How many a sad and weary-hearted wife I can think of, whose feeble hands have long since failed in the effort to hold up the standard alone. Her husband and children have the controlling influence, and you would not know that she was still trying to think herself a Christian, if you did not see her now and then wending her lonely way to the Communion table!

Yet, supposing the probabilities were much stronger than they are that your good influence would be greater over an impenitent husband, than his evil influence over you, still you know we must never do evil that good may come. If a young lady does not succeed in leading her friend to Christ before marriage, how can she expect to after? Or rather, why not defer both engagement and marriage till their hearts have become one in the Lord?

"Be not unequally yoked together with unbelievers; for what fellowship hath righteousness with unrighteousness? and what communion hath light with darkness? and what concord hath Christ with Belial? and what agreement hath the temple of God with idols?" 2 Cor. 6: 14, 15, 16.

You will say, no doubt, as the young ladies of my Bible Class did, that such a marriage does not seem right, and yet perhaps like them you may not be quite prepared to pronounce it wrong. There is a secret unwillingness in the minds of most young persons to commit themselves on this point; but it appears to me of the utmost importance that they should do so—that it should be a settled matter with them, a fixed principle, so that they shall be beyond the reach of temptation. This must be done before their affections are enlisted, for after that, it will be difficult for them to look at the subject impartially.

Here allow me to bring up again a principle of action alluded to in a previous letter. If any given course seems to you wrong, or even *doubtful*, for you it is wrong. "To him that thinketh a thing unclean to him it is unclean." We are not at liberty to do anything till we are sure it is right. "He that doubteth is damned if he eat, because he eateth not of faith." "Whatsoever is not of faith is sin." Anything, however innocent in others, is wrong in you, until you are convinced in your own mind that it is right, and that God calls you to it. This important principle, if faithfully applied, will settle many a case of conscience. You perhaps wish to do certain things which others do, but are not quite sure it would be right; then you may be quite sure that for you it would be wrong.

Does this rule seem too strict? It is not stricter than perfect love will dictate. Ask your own heart. You love your earthly father very much; it has ever been your study to please him; you carefully avoid, not only what he has positively forbidden, but everything that you so much as suspect would be disagreeable to him. You do not think of stopping to inquire whether your brothers and sisters do these doubtful things. Now, if you love your Heavenly Father as you do your earthly parent, you will preserve the same course in regard to Him.

There are some Christians who will tell you that they don't believe it is wrong for pious persons to marry the impenitent. But ask them *if they are sure it is right*, and I think most of them would hesitate. Such marriages have ever been a fruitful source of evil. They have done much to lower the standard of piety in the church. I would earnestly say to all young Christians, as you value your happiness for life, as you value your usefulness in the church, and in the world, as you value your Christian influence, as you value your own sanctification, as you value the approving smile and blessing of God, "*Be not unequally yoked together with unbelievers.*"

Yours in the best of bonds.

LETTER XI.

CONVERSATION.

She openeth her mouth with wisdom, and in her tongue is the law of kindness.—PROV. 31 : 26.

Dear Eugenia,—When we give ourselves to God we dedicate our *conversational powers* to Him. It is a question of the greatest interest how we may use them entirely for his glory. Much of life being necessarily spent in conversation, how important that it be of the right stamp! When it is not what it should be, (and alas, this is too generally the case,) we pervert a noble gift, besides wasting our Lord's time. Each day brings with it golden opportunities of doing good by *conversation*; how shall the young Christian be prepared to improve them?

The first and most important requisite is *a holy heart*. "For out of the abundance of the heart the mouth speaketh." One whose thoughts and feelings are occupied with divine things cannot afford to trifle or gossip. One who loves God will love his fellow-men, and cannot afford to slander, or speak evil of them. Those in whose heart the love of God and men prevails will naturally—we should almost say necessarily—avoid the numerous faults which are observable in the intercourse of worldly persons. Their speech will "be always with grace seasoned with salt." They will continually look to the Lord for direction, and will continually receive it. Wherever they are—at home, abroad, by the fireside, and the wayside—they will be intent on imparting and obtaining good. They will stir one another up to duty, and comfort one another with the comfort wherewith they themselves are comforted of God. They will admonish one another daily, will rebuke and reprove with all long-suffering. When they meet with a brother who has been overtaken in a fault, they will restore such a one in the spirit of meekness. The impenitent they will converse with faithfully and tenderly. Many who call themselves Christians feel a great reluctance to the performance of this duty, and on various pretexts excuse themselves from it. But those who are wholly given up to God—who love Him with all their hearts, have no diffiuclty. The love of Christ and the love of souls constrain them to speak. It is not done from a sense of duty, but from a holy sympathy with the sinner and with God. Now, I do not like to urge it on you as a *duty* to converse faithfully with the impenitent, whenever and wherever opportunity is given, for if you attempted it *on this ground* I should not anticipate any good results. There is a wide difference between conversing with an impenitent person simply to ease your own conscience, and warning him out of the fulness of an affectionate heart. I would say to all young Christians, "Be filled with the Spirit," and then you cannot help speaking.

It is not always necessary, nor is it always expedient, to say a great deal to unconverted persons. Frequently a word, expressive of your deep and tender interest—anything which conveys the idea that you are feeling and praying for them, will suffice. It is like a nail in a sure place. You then become to them "a living epistle," for every time they see you, they will think—"There is one who cares for my soul—who is earnestly desirous of my salvation—ought I not to care for it too?" Thus you will be preaching to them when you are not aware of it. Many persons excuse themselves from this duty on the plea of unfitness. They think they have no talent for conversation, that they cannot present the subject judiciously, cannot meet objections, and shall be likely to make mistakes. Undoubtedly some are better qualified than others, but let all do what they can. Generally it is not argument that is wanted. Let your friend know that you consider him in danger, that you feel for him, and want to save him, and with the divine blessing it will awaken his feelings, and this is usually what is needed. Let his heart become softened, and he is prepared to receive the truth.

Still, in order to be qualified for the highest usefulness to such persons, you must try to become acquainted with the best methods of approaching their minds, and the proper way of meeting their objections. With this in view, listen attentively to your pastor, when he addresses the unconverted, and read on the subject, continually keeping in use the thoughts thus gained.

Perhaps you will say, " I am young, and it seems for the present proper that I should retain the attitude of a learner, rather than to be assuming that of a teacher."

The adversary suggests this, because he knows that nothing will help you forward so fast, as the continual effort to communicate what you learn. "Give, and it shall be given you; good measure, pressed down, and shaken together, and running over, shall men give into your bosom." This is pre-eminently true in regard to imparting spiritual treasures. Use your light, and you shall have more—put it under a bushel, and it will go out.

When you meet with Christians, endeavor to draw from them some account of their religious experience, and speak freely of your own. In this way you may do much to strengthen the faith of God's dear children. No matter if they are older than yourself, and have been longer on the way; do not on that account wait for them to speak first. To strengthen the faith of Christians, and promote holiness of heart and life, appears to me even more important than making direct efforts for the salvation of the impenitent. For when the church comes right, the world will follow. Such labors, therefore, though indirect, may be regarded as the most efficient means of saving the unconverted.

Now, my dear Eugenia, if by the grace of God you have learned what it is to be entirely consecrated, and what it is to appropriate the promises, you are in that attitude where the Lord can use you for the good of others. You will find comparatively few in the church at present who have much experimental knowledge of these things. Tell them what God has done for you, and it will be to them a very powerful kind of preaching. Nothing preaches so convincingly and efficaciously as experience. When you meet with Christians who know the full blessedness of the life of faith, then hasten to draw from them the riches of their past and present experience, for your own benefit and encouragement.

In this way will your conversation be as becometh saints. The Spirit will speak through you to others, and through them again to you. Every one you meet is either a saint or a sinner; you have a message to both; lose no time, but be about your Father's business. I would not, however, be understood to say that there must never be any time given to ordinary topics—never anything said in a playful way, with a view of diffusing cheerfulness through the family circle, or raising the spirits of the care-worn and depressed—all these things have their appropriate place, and the indwelling Spirit will not fail to check you when you are in danger of going too far.

People generally seem to think that when together they must talk all the time. Whenever a pause occurs in the conversation, they hasten to fill it up with something—no matter what. In this way a great deal is said that had much better have been left unsaid. Now, it appears to me that occasional pauses, even of considerable length, so far from being unpleasant or unsuitable, may be very serviceable, affording time to commune with God, and listen to the Inward Voice. If we would have the Lord direct the conversation, we should give Him time to speak, or rather give ourselves time to hear. I do not think the time is lost when there is a pause in a conference meeting, or in a social interview—certainly not among spiritual persons. It would be well for those who so eagerly fill up every gap in the conversation with whatever comes to hand, to inquire whether a few moments of "inward recollection" might not be more profitable.

The subject of *Conversation* is an interesting, because a practical one—a matter which comes up every day and every hour. It is of the utmost importance that young Christians should be careful here, or they will be continually bringing themselves into condemnation. May you have grace to order your conversation aright. Let your manner be calm and deliberate, courteous, gentle, and kind. Do not speak loud or fast. Listen attentively to others, and never interrupt them. "The crowning grace of conversation is, *to listen well.*" Present the good thoughts which may be given you in appropriate language, and let there be that in all you say, both as regards the matter and the manner, which shall come up to the idea conveyed in the beautiful words of Moses, "My speech shall distil as the dew."—Deut. 32 : 2.

Yours in the best of bonds.

LETTER XII.

READING.

Dear Eugenia,—Solomon said, "Of making books there is no end." Of the truth of this assertion we have abundant evidence. Books of all sorts, to say nothing of papers and periodicals, are so rapidly issuing from the press, that it would be impossible to keep up with the literature of the day, even if we did nothing else but read. As most of us have a great many other things to do, it becomes an important inquiry, by what rules we shall be guided in making a selection from the mass of reading matter which presents itself.

The books that young people read have perhaps as much influence in the formation of their character as the companions with whom they associate. There are, therefore, the same reasons for being careful in the selection, and much the same rules will apply in both cases. Let me know what company a young person keeps, and what books he reads, and it is easy to judge what he is now, and is likely to be through life. I know not how it may be with others, but I am sure that in my own case the books I read in early life had a far greater influence over me than my associates.

In choosing your books let me remind you again that *you are not your own.* You are not at liberty to read every entertaining thing that comes in your way, but you must first ask permission of your Divine Master. It will not do to waste His time in reading something that is merely entertaining. You have now begun to live in earnest, and I trust will do nothing great or small for which you cannot render a reason. You are now to live by the moment, and the continual inquiry with you is to be, "Lord, what wilt thou have me to do?" Anything which after making this inquiry you honestly believe He would have you to read, read—*and nothing else.* Avoid everything about which you are in the least doubtful; it may do for others, but not for you; it may do for you at some future time, but not now. And here you have a rule which will enable you to decide in regard to fictitious reading. Undoubtedly most of the works of fiction would thus be banished from your table.

In the morning of each day you ask the Holy Spirit to guide you in all things; the language of your heart is

"Direct, control, suggest this day,
All I design, or do, or say."

Now every time you turn aside to read a story, or do anything else simply for your own gratification, without stopping to ask whether it will be pleasing to God, that moment you desert your Guide.

You will find many professed disciples who allow themselves in light reading; they will tell you they don't see any harm in it; but you have given yourself *wholly* to God, and put yourself *wholly* under his direction, therefore the opinions and practices of others are no rule for you. Besides, a deeply spiritual person cannot enjoy such reading, and if you should find a taste for it reviving, it would be time to inquire whether you had not lost ground in the heavenly race. A Christian who is really hungering and thirsting after righteousness delights so much in the Bible, and those books which breathe its spirit, that light literature loses its charms for him.

While you follow the Inward Voice you will find yourself led to read those books only which are calculated to fit you for the service of God. Of course they will not be exclusively religious, because while on earth you need various kinds of knowledge in order to be fitted for the various duties of life. Perhaps, too, it will sometimes be needful for you to read for recreation, but there is even then no occasion to resort to fiction, for you will find plenty of works in which entertainment and instruction are happily blended.

You will perhaps think, as most people do, that some fictitious reading may be allowed. As much as you please, provided only you have permission from the Heavenly Guide, and are *sure* you have it.

There is a class of Christians addressed in the eighth verse of the thirty-second Psalm, who walk in the light of love, and are easily led. God says to such in this verse, "I will instruct thee and teach thee in the way thou shalt go, I will guide thee with mine eye." There is another and quite a different class addressed in the next verse; they are persons who are always crawling on the ground, feeling for the dividing line between Christ and the world.

The question what is right and what is wrong means with them, "How far may we venture to go in the forbidden direction?" To such God says, "Be ye not as the horse or the mule which have no understanding: whose mouth must be held in with bit and bridle." These persons are *legalists;* they have no understanding of the life of faith, and the sweetly constraining power of love; nothing but the restraints of law will hold them in.

You must not only take heed *what* you read, but also *how* you read. Do not read too much, nor too fast. This you will be continually tempted to do; but nothing is gained by it. Johnson says, "Whatever is worth reading once, is worth reading twice." Books have multiplied so much since his day, that I doubt if he would have the resolution to adhere to his own rule. I believe, however, that six books read twice, will be worth more to us than twelve read once. I often find a third and even a fourth reading advantageous. Read till you make the author's thoughts your own, and then secure them by putting them to use. I find, in reading religious writings of a practical or experimental kind, that the thoughts must not only be weighed and received, but *acted upon*, otherwise I am likely to let them slip.

I hope you have no ambition to be what is called *a great reader*. Such a reputation is generally acquired at the expense of other things more important.

Duties never conflict. The monitor within will not call you to read when you should be doing something else. Never allow yourself to read when in your own soul you believe you ought to be praying, meditating, or acting. So sure as you do, although it should be the best book in the world, you will bring yourself into condemnation, for it is certain that you are then seeking your own gratification instead of the approval of God.

We often hear people regretting that they have not more time to read. This is wrong. God gives us all the time for that, and other enjoyments, which is best, and the Christian who is saying daily and hourly, "Lord what wilt *thou* have me to do?" goes cheerfully forward in the way marked out for him, and finds no room in his heart for regrets.

Perhaps you will say, "I desire to be directed by the Spirit *what* to read, *how* to read, and *when* to read, but I am not always sure I understand the intimations of his will." I can at least tell you when you may be sure that you are *not* following it:

1. When you read books, periodicals, and papers, which are not calculated to be beneficial to you.

2. When you read simply for your own gratification, or to make a display of the knowledge acquired.

3. When you read too much, or too fast, and without suitable care to profit by what you read.

4. When you read to the neglect of other duties.

I cannot leave this subject without earnestly commending the BIBLE to you as the book of all books. Do not let other reading encroach upon it. This you will be continually tempted to do. Other books may be read—this must be studied. Drink deep into its spirit. Read it daily—not as a duty, but as a delight. Read it as you would a letter from a dear friend; it is a letter from your dearest Friend, and it is filled with love. Study it faithfully—constantly—but never to all eternity will your mind be able to grasp its full, deep meaning!

LETTER XIII.

OCCUPATIONS.

Dear Eugenia,—You feel that the choice of *occupations* is a subject of great importance. It is so. How we shall fill up our time to the best advantage, is a question of much interest. *Our* time did I say? No, not *ours;* that time which the Lord gave, and which we have given back to Him. When we gave ourselves to God, we consecrated all our time, and now we wish to use every moment for Him. It will be taking that which is not ours, or, as the Scriptures express it, *robbing God*, if we use any of his time for our own gratification merely, or the gratification of others, without permission; if we waste it in unnecessary sleep, or recreation, in trifling conversation, or trifling books, or any occupation in which He does not call us to engage. The truly consecrated Christian never has any lost time; he is always about his Father's business, and when his thoughts are not necessarily engaged about other things, prayer, praise, and heavenly meditation fill up the intervals.

The great rule in regard to our occupations is, to follow the leadings of the Spirit and Providence of God. These will always point the same way, and always harmonise with the word. Having given ourselves to God, we must let him have control of all our movements. We have no more right to choose our own occupations, than we have to be idle. It is not enough that we are always busy about something—even though it be a very good thing—we are to be doing just that, and that only, which our Master calls us to do.

There are some kinds of work which you like, and others that you do not like. These likes and dislikes must not be allowed any weight; the only question is "Lord, what wilt thou have me to do?" How pleasant it is to work for God! The truly consecrated soul has no other work. The wife of President Edwards, who had a remarkably deep and rich experience in divine things, used to say, "O, how good is it to work for God in the day-time, and at night to lie down under his smiles." The common or ordinary business of everyday life is dignified and ennobled by being brought out and done under His eye, at His command, to His glory.

You remember Newton said that if two angels should be sent into this world, one to rule an empire, and the other to sweep a chimney, they would not have the least choice. This brings out the true idea of the way in which everything should be done—so fully *in* God and *for* God.

Perhaps you say, "This is no more than I should expect of angels, but it is too high a standard for me." No higher than the standard of the Bible. God requires you to be as good as an angel. I think I hear you exclaim, "As good as an angel? why, that is impossible!" How good is an angel? As good as he can be, and you are required to be as good as you can be. All intelligent beings, from the little child to the archangel, give satisfaction to their Creator when they love Him with their whole hearts, and fill up their little measure of duty according to their several abilities. "The perfection of a circle," Hannah More says, "consists not in its dimensions, but in its completeness."

I have often found it profitable to inquire how an angel would probably act, if placed in my circumstances, and then try to do just that which I should expect him to do. Now in regard to this matter of *employments*, I would have you, like the angels, do what the Lord gives you to do,

> "With a glad heart and free."

Do it *because He gives it*, rather than because it is agreeable or important, or somebody expects it, or it will give others a good opinion of you. These inferior motives you would think unworthy of an angel; then they are unworthy of a Christain.

You will find many *domestic duties* devolving upon you. Perhaps you have no taste for these employments, and are ready to call them drudgery. But no—the view we have just taken raises them to a level with the most dignified occupations of life. The Saviour says, "Whether ye eat or drink, *or whatever you do*, do all to the glory of God." This certainly takes in the whole list of household duties, down to the smallest and most ignoble.

Seeing a great part of life is necessarily taken up with little things, what a comfort and satisfaction it is to know that God and religion need not be shut out from one of them! Sweep your floor just as Newton's angel would sweep his chimney. He would do it well—he would do it cheerfully;—and when he got to the top, you might hear him singing, "Glory to God in the highest, on earth peace, good will to men!"

I believe you think *sewing* rather a dull employment, compared with study, writing, and many other things. I am much of your opinion; and therefore we will do no more of it than is necessary. It is enough to make one's heart ache to see how much time is wasted in *useless needle-work*—trimmings, embroidery, rug-work, fancy-netting, &c, I can call it nothing but busy idleness. What should you think to see an angel doing such work? How then can a Christian do it? Such employments may answer to amuse invalids, and children, and those who can do nothing better. Many good people will tell you there is no harm in such things—that they like to do them—and they don't believe it is wrong. I can only say, that we are here, as in other things, to follow our Guide. He will not call us to do anything of this kind, until every duty, personal and relative, is fairly discharged. When you have done all that belongs to you at home and abroad, and all that is desirable in regard to your own intellectual and spiritual improvement, *if there is any time left*, you may find yourself called to take up with some of these forms of elegant idleness.

Much time is consumed by our young people in Music and Drawing, and often to little purpose. Where there is a decided talent for these pursuits, and the arrangements of Providence favor its cultivation, and the young Christian is clear in her own mind that she is called to it, and that it is just the appropriation of time which under the circumstances will be most pleasing to God, then she may engage in these things with a clear conscience, and find a blessing in them.

Perhaps it will become necessary for you to support yourself by your own exertions. The spirit of entire consecration will require and enable you to enter with cheerfulness and alacrity upon any course of labor to which you may be called. While you work hard to procure food, clothing, and shelter, these will not be the primary objects in your mind; you are living for God, and you will attend to these things because He requires it, and your object will be, not personal comfort, but to keep yourself in good working order for his service.

Some very foolish people fancy that labor is degrading; but our Saviour, by saying, "*Whatever you do,* do all to the glory of God," has forever ennobled it. Do it to thy glory? May we—can we—thus glorify Thee? Then are all kinds of labor by that one word of thine made truly noble!

After you have fully met the claims of duty at home, there will be many demands upon you from other quarters. You must visit the poor, watch with the sick, and comfort the afflicted. You may also do much good with your *pen,*—writing letters, and contributing to religious papers and periodicals. In this way you can impart to others the valuable thoughts which may be given to you, and thus continue to do good on earth long after you have gone to heaven. It is said of David that, "having served his own generation by the will of God he fell on sleep." He not only "served *his own* generation," during a long and active life, but through his *pen* he has been serving every generation since.

When you put a useful thought on paper there is no knowing how widely its good influence may be felt. Long after your tongue is silent in the grave, it may be said, "She being dead yet speaketh." Madame Guyon lived and wrote two hundred years ago, but her work is not yet done. She still goes from house to house (not only in her native land, but in England and America), with a noiseless tread, and a silent voice, which the heart hears—pleading with Christians to be holy, and in her own example holding up to them a standard of piety, which the Church has well nigh lost sight of. How interesting it is to think of one, who has been so many years in heaven, still gliding about among us, repeating the words of love and wisdom which she uttered in life!

Perhaps you doubt your ability to write. Be holy, and such thoughts shall be given you as God can and will use for the good of others.

There is another class of duties, growing out of your relations to the church. You must aid in the

Sabbath School, the Prayer Meetings, and benevolent associations, and do every thing which God shall permit towards fulfilling the promise you make, whenever a new member is added, to "watch over them, and seek their edification." You may do much in this way, especially among the young. Then there is a large number of unconverted persons in the congregation with whom you worship. They are looking to the members of the church to do something for their salvation. They have a claim on your sympathy, prayers, and benevolent effort. Here is a wide field of labor. All Christians should consider themselves called to be *Missionaries;* and if not sent to the foreign field, they are to labor at home. If we feel right, the love of Christ constraineth us to work as diligently, and as faithfully, as if we were under special appointment.

Do we not hear a voice ever saying to us, "Go work in my vineyard?" O yes; and this work—what is it? A blessed privilege—a refreshment to the soul—a perpetual means of growth—an opportunity of expressing our love, which the full heart craves!

O let us enter eagerly into all these ways of serving our Lord. Instead of dragging ourselves along by a sense of duty, we will give Him our time, talents, strength, property—all we have, and all we are—in the same spirit that Mary poured her box of spikenard on His feet. Then that cold word *duty* will be forgotten, and the sweet word LOVE will take its place!

Ever yours.

THE ELIXIR.

I.

Teach me, my God and King,
In all things thee to see;
And, what I do in anything,
To do it as for thee:

II.

Not rudely, as a beast,
To run into an action;
But still to make thee prepossessed,
And give it his perfection.

III.

A man that looks on glass,
On it may stay his eye;
Or if he pleaseth, through it pass,
And then the heaven espy.

IV.

All may of thee partake:
Nothing can be so mean,
Which with this tincture, FOR THY SAKE,
Will not grow bright and clean.

V.

A servant, with this clause,
Makes drudgery divine;
Who sweeps a room, as for thy laws,
Makes that, and th' action, fine.

VI.

This is the famous stone,
That turneth all to gold;
For that, which God doth touch and own,
Cannot for less be told.

GEORGE HERBERT, 1630.

LETTER XIV.

SOCIAL DUTIES.

Dear Eugenia,—In addition to those duties which lie more immediately between your own soul and God, the occupations that tend to your spiritual and intellectual improvement, and those which pertain to the comfort and welfare of the family, there is another class of duties, growing out of your relations to *society.* If you should be so intent on your own intellectual and spiritual progress as to neglect family duties, it would certainly deserve no better name than selfishness. But those who suffer themselves to be entirely engrossed by their own families are equally open to the charge of selfishness.

There is something so very absorbing in the cares devolving on a young wife and mother, that she needs to be on her guard, lest all her energies and sympathies should be contracted within the magic circle of *home.* Many a woman is lost to society after she becomes the head of a family. But this should not be. Her family must of course make large demands on her time, thoughts, and affections, but should by no means be permitted to take all.

Many seem to think that faithfully to discharge domestic duties is all that should be required of them, and all they can do. In some cases we might think so too (especially where, as we often see, the strength is small, and the demands upon it large), were it not that, let circumstances be ever so unfavorable, we always find a truly devoted Christian woman will make her influence felt beyond her own family circle. She feels for others; and feeling for them, she will think and act for them, to the extent of her ability. It is matter of thankfulness that while so many women, like Martha, are cumbered with much serving—careful and troubled about many things which are quite superfluous, there are some of a different stamp. While they love their own families, and take all needful care of them, they can love God's family also, and do good to every member of it as they have opportunity.

I have in my mind now an individual, who makes

her influence felt in the church and neighborhood to a remarkable extent. She has been several years a widow, and earns with her own hands a subsistence for her children; yet I know of no one who is more faithful in the discharge of *Social Duties.* She is constant and punctual in her attendance on all the religious meetings, and the Sabbath School, distributes tracts, watches with the sick, visits the poor and afflicted, and where she cannot reach the case herself, calls in the aid of others. Yet her health is not remarkably vigorous, nor has she any uncommon abilities; almost anybody else could do what she does, if they only had as large a heart. If any woman might be justified in spending all her time and energies at home, we should say this poor widow might; but she loves God—and all the human family, for His sake—and to do them good always presents itself to her mind in the light of a privilege more than a duty.

You may be a good daughter and sister, a devoted wife and mother—you may be quite self-sacrificing in these relations, and yet be *intensely selfish.* The world loves *its own.*

Let us now take a glance at some of the more mportant *Social Duties.*

1st. *The various Social Meetings* have a claim upon your attention. There is or ought to be a Prayer Meeting among the sisters of the church to which you belong. This is a blessed means of grace and should on no account be neglected. When the Providence of God permits, be constant and punctual in your attendance, and ever ready to bear a part in sustaining it. Be free to speak and pray as opportunity shall be given, without waiting for some one else to do it better. Do not talk of want of ability; all the ability required is a heart full of faith and love. The reflex of influence of these exercises on your own soul will be most beneficial, besides the direct good done to others. You will be an immense loser if you hang back from these duties. Do not wait for older Christians to go forward; begin while you are young; if you do not, the probability is that you never will begin.

2. *The Sabbath School* opens to you another field of usefulness, and here again the reflex influence will abundantly repay the time and strength you expend. To be a Sabbath School Teacher is to be a Pastor on a small scale. You have the care of immortal souls; solemn is the responsibility, and sweet the reward connected with this work. Do not be satisfied with interesting and instructing your pupils; rest not till they are converted; and rest not then, till they are sanctified wholly. It is pleasant work, and very important work, to feed the lambs.

3. *Benevolent Associations* will claim a share of your attention. Do with your might what your

hands finds to do in this department of labor, and the blessing of many ready to perish shall come upon you. I know it often requires a great effort to leave the occupations at home in which you are interested, and go out in uncomfortable weather, it may be, and when, perhaps, your head aches, or you are tired—to attend this Sewing Circle, and that Board Meeting, or carry round a subscription paper—but still, if you are not sure that your duty lies at home, you will be a gainer by the sacrifice; good will be accomplished, a worthy example set to others, a salutary influence exerted, and God honored in the sight of the world.

Do not excuse yourself on the plea that there are others who have more leisure, or greater ablities; you can never delegate *your* duty to another; no one can do *your* work for you. Whether others do little or much, may you have grace so to meet all the responsibilities of life, that it can be truthfully engraven on your tomb,—"She hath done what she could."

4. *Visiting the poor, the sick, the aged, and the afflicted*, stands prominent on the list of *Social Duties*. Carry to them such relief as may be within your reach, and especially carry to them the consolations of the Gospel. Many a rich lesson will you learn in these visits; and if you go with a heart in sympathy with them, and with God, it is not possible

to estimate the comfort and religious benefit you may impart. Such persons are generally quite secluded, and the sight of a friendly face does them good. They will be likely to encroach on your time and patience by going into the narration of all their troubles. But do not consider it a loss of time to attend to these unimportant details. It is worth a great deal to them to get a kind and sympathising listener, and pouring out their griefs lightens the load. Sometimes they will not give you opportunity to say much; no matter—you have comforted them not a little simply by *listening*. Pray with them, if permitted, and give or lend appropriate tracts and books.

5. *Social Visiting* among friends and neighbors must come in for its share of attention. It is obvious that this affords opportunity of doing much good. Alas, that it should be so generally perverted to frivolity and worldliness! Going into company will not hurt you, provided you go in the same spirit that your Master did—intent on doing good. Always ask Him to go with you, and make the conversation profitable—cherishing at the same time a confidence that He will. If you suffer the time to slip away in unprofitable discourse you will grieve the Spirit, and be likely to bring your soul into darkness and condemnation, besides losing a golden opportunity to benefit others. Do not let the example

of older Christians influence you here. It is no rule for you. When all Christians come to be holy—fully given up to God—what a change will be manifested in our social gatherings! Now they talk of everything but Christ; then the language of their hearts will be,

> "We only wish to speak of Him,
> Who lived, and died, and reigns for us."

If you are fond of book and pen, you will be tempted to neglect these *Social Duties.* It will require no small effort for you to leave your favorite occupations—occupations which elevate the mind and improve the heart—to mingle with people who seem to be absorbed in the cares and pleasures of this life. If you are refined in your taste and feelings, intent on self-improvement, you will be tempted to avoid the society of those who do not sympathise with you. But this will never do. Wherever you go, there are two objects before you—to *give*, and to *receive.* By the Divine blessing you may always do the one or the other. Therefore, instead of turning coldly away from the frivolous, the worldly, and the uninteresting mingle freely with them, as the providence and Spirit of God shall direct, and in the same temper with which the Saviour sat at meat with publicans and sinners.

You would like to build a castle, as a romantic friend of mine once said,

"To shut out the wicked, the stupid, and rude,
And let in the witty, the wise, and the good."

But remember your high calling; remember our Lord Jesus, who left the glorious society of Heaven, to live more than thirty-three years among those who were utterly incapable of appreciating Him. It was only here and there that He met with one who could have any sympathy with Him at all. Now what would you have thought, if, instead of going from place to place, teaching and healing the multitudes, he had been in the habit of stealing away to Bethany, and spending the principal part of his time in the luxury of refined, intellectual, and Christian intercourse with those whom He loved best—Lazarus and John, Martha and Mary? "The servant is not greater than his Lord." Mingle in the world, and bear with it, as He did; labor for it, and bless it, as He did: that at last you may be able to say with Him, "I have finished the work which Thou gavest me to do."

"She who thus marks from day to day;
With generous acts her radiant way,
Treads the same path the Saviour trod,
The path to glory and to God."

LETTER XV.

DRESS.

"Why take ye thought for raiment?"—CHRIST.

Dear Eugenia,—Custom or fashion seems to bear sway in many things, but in nothing perhaps more tyrannically than in the matter of *dress*. Manifold are the inconveniences and discomforts submitted to under its iron rule. The children of the world are slaves to fashion; but Christians have a right to break away from this thraldom. The Saviour says to them, "Ye are not of the world, but I have chosen you out of the world." It is their privilege now to unloose the bands of their neck, and be slaves no more.

I trust you are not one of those who think that *dress* is too small a matter to bring your religion to bear upon. Nothing is small or unimportant which can draw us into sin. And we know that dress is not beneath the notice of God, for he has repeatedly alluded to it in His word. You remember that remarkable inventory in Isaiah 3 : 18–23. We see from this that the Lord takes notice of every article we wear.

Individuals sometimes turn away impatiently from

Gospel; and gently whispers, "The poor ye have always with you." The world says you should at least wear what is becoming to your rank in life—that you need not be too scrupulous about ornament—that you must not be singularly plain, &c., but Christ says, "Be not conformed to the world."

Do not give any more attention to dress than you honestly believe *comfort* and *propriety* require. If you do more than this, it involves a waste of *time*, *money*, and *thought*—three things which you have solemnly dedicated to God, and therefore have no liberty to waste. Moreover, it will nourish pride and vanity, weaken your influence as a Christian, be a bad example to others, and be contrary to the Scripture rule. See 1 Peter, 3 : 3. 1 Tim. 2 : 9.

Some people are conscientious about spending *money* for superfluities, but they take their Lord's *time* without any scruple. They will not purchase trimmings and finery, but at a great expense of time and thought they will *make* these things, and then congratulate themselves on their economy! *Time*, *thought*, and *money* are three talents given us for the service of God, and we have no more right to waste one than the other. I am utterly at a loss to understand how that young lady can believe herself to be a true Christian—living for God—when she spends hour after hour, and day after day, in embroidering and ornamenting her dresses. Is this walking worthy of her high calling? What can she say in defence of such a practice? She can say she is only doing as other people do. What a common excuse, and what a miserable one! Is this the Bible standard? Is this being a Bible Christian? She says perhaps she is only gratifying her own taste, and pleasing her friends. She would probably come nearer the truth if she said it was to gratify her own pride and vanity. But even taking her version of it, has she not got away from the Bible standard, which says we are not to please ourselves? and as to our friends, we must hate them; that is, whenever their claims conflict with the claims of God, we are to act as if we hated them.

In all that we do, we should be mindful of the power of our example. I know an excellent Christian lady, who has ample means, and ample leisure at command, but she will not purchase rich clothing, nor spend time in ornamenting her dress, because others around her, who could not so well spare either time or money, would be led into temptation by her example; some committing sin by imitating her, and others by repining at their inability to do so. You see she is acting on Paul's principle of genuine benevolence—she will not eat meat, if it shall cause others to offend. This is generous—this looks like loving your neighbor as yourself. How all the petty excuses for self-indulgence quail before it.

walking worthy of her high calling? What can she say in defence of such a practice? She can say she is only doing as other people do. What a common excuse, and what a miserable one! Is this the Bible standard? Is this being a Bible Christian? She says perhaps she is only gratifying her own taste, and pleasing her friends. She would probably come nearer the truth if she said it was to gratify her own pride and vanity. But even taking her version of it, has she not got away from the Bible standard, which says we are not to please ourselves? and as to our friends, we must hate them; that is, whenever their claims conflict with the claims of God, we are to act as if we hated them.

In all that we do, we should be mindful of the power of our example. I know an excellent Christian lady, who has ample means, and ample leisure at command, but she will not purchase rich clothing, nor spend time in ornamenting her dress, because others around her, who could not so well spare either time or money, would be led into temptation by her example; some committing sin by imitating her, and others by repining at their inability to do so. You see she is acting on Paul's principle of genuine benevolence—she will not eat meat, if it shall cause others to offend. This is generous—this looks like loving your neighbor as yourself. How all the petty excuses for self-indulgence quail before it.

A very important consideration against giving time, money, and thought to dress, is that *it weakens your influence as a Christian.* "No man liveth to himself." You are a living epistle, known and read of all men; now if the first page they read strikes them unfavorably, the rest will not be likely to have much weight. How can you expect to persuade any one to renounce the world, when a glance at your fashionable apparel convinces them that you have not yet renounced it yourself? How can you expect to succeed in winning a half-hearted disciple to a life of entire consecration, when your outward adorning tells too truly that you have never yet laid all on the altar? You may speak of the enjoyment you find in religion, but it will have little effect while your style of dress betrays the fact that your heart is, to say the least, divided between God and the world.

In order to have your influence over others all that it should be, it is not enough that you cannot be called *decidedly dressy*, you must be *decidedly plain.* It must be apparent that nothing has been sought but *comfort* and *propriety.* Anything beyond this will weaken your influence wonderfully. You may be satisfied of that by observing your own feelings in regard to others who err in this respect. You can cast the mantle of charity over them, but it is impossible to feel that they are dead to the world.

Now your personal influence as a Christian is a thing too valuable to be thus lightly thrown away.

It will not do for you to say, "It is nobody's business how I dress." People will make it their business to observe and comment upon it. You must remember that many persons are weak minded, and make much of trifles. Paul's rule (which indeed is only the working out of Christian love) forbids you to indulge in anything, however innocent, that will make one of the weak ones to offend, or be offended.

You think you could go to a martyr's stake. I presume you could. But there are some things in life which require more courage than that; one is, to dare to be singular; and another is, to make thorough work in the matter of crucifying self.

You ask whether a Christian is required to dispense with ornaments entirely? It appears to me that the principles we have adopted would banish them altogether—at least in the present state of the world. Most church members in our cities and large towns have departed so widely, in this particular, from Christian simplicity, that it behoves those who would keep themselves unspotted from the world—those who would raise the tone of piety in the Church—those who would be holy—to take a decided stand against all appearance of evil here. Let it be evident that you are *dead*. Remember the Saviour says to his disciples, "Ye are the salt of the earth." Observe, he does not say you *ought* to be, but you *are*. Now, if by the indulgence of your taste for dress (even in what would generally be considered a very moderate degree,—that is, by allowing anything beyond comfort and propriety), you diminish your power over the minds of others, *the salt has lost its savor.*

You feel that you have given yourself to the Lord without reserve, and now your great work is to persuade others, both in the Church and out of it, to do the same. If there is anything in the present mode of dress which you have reason to think will weaken your influence with any of these minds, Christian love requires you to drop it at once. Are you not willing to go dressed very plainly, if it will help you to save souls? That it will, there can be no doubt.

Let us "be clothed with humility," and wear always that *ornament* which in the sight of God is of great price."

Yours affectionately.

LETTER XVI.

HEALTH.

Dear Eugenia,—You will smile, perhaps, at the caption of this letter, and ask me if it is one of th-duties of a young Christian to be healthy! I am not sure that I should be far wrong if I answered in the affirmative. Not that you have this matter entirely in your own hands—but certainly you have to a great extent. Within a few years much light has been thrown on the laws of our physical nature, and with light there always comes responsibility. Our fathers and mothers sinned ignorantly, yet they were punished; how much more shall we deserve to suffer if we sin wilfully!

Health is a thing of inestimable value as it stands connected with our enjoyment and our usefulness. All acknowledge this, yet how little most people are willing to do to preserve it! I often notice with surprise that while they will submit to painful and expensive remedies, and compass sea and land to recover health, when once it is lost, they will not submit to a little self-denial in obedience to physical laws, in order to retain it. How few you find who are living *right* in regard to health! They have plenty of excuses to offer for this neglect, but these excuses will not prevent the evil consequences. Punishment follows transgression, though not always immediately. The author of "Lacon" remarks, "The excesses of our youth are drafts upon our old age, payable thirty years after date." But "because sentence against an evil work is not executed speedily therefore the heart of the sons of men is fully set in them to do evil." Physical laws are as much the ordinances of God as moral laws. The fact that a breach of them, even when committed in ignorance, is followed by suffering, seems to show that there is sin in it.

Among medical writers there are many different theories in regard to the means of *restoring* health, but there is a remarkable unanimity of opinion as to the best way of *preserving* it. They all unite in recommending *air*, *exercise*, and *temperance*. Now if we shut ourselves up the principal part of the day, and all night, in close rooms, with little or no exercise, and allow ourselves to partake freely of unwholesome food, we are sinning against light. Certainly the civilised world abounds in such sinners. To "come out and be separate" demands more courage and self-denial than most people possess. You know it is a much higher evidence of grace to keep on, day after day, doing exactly right in every little thing, than occasionally to perform illustrious and magnanimous actions.

I would not have you seek the preservation of health chiefly for the pleasure and comfort of feeling well. You have a higher reason than this for obeying the laws of your nature, viz., to keep yourself in good working order for the service of God. If He weakens your strength in the way, and sets you aside from active employment, it is your duty and privilege to submit cheerfully, and even to rejoice in it as an expression of His will; but you have no right to set yourself aside.

We see many good people who appear to be exhausting themselves in their efforts to serve the Lord. They have become so deeply interested in some particular form of benevolent action that they press forward with the greatest ardor, and neglect to take proper care of their health. In this they are probably wrong. Sometimes no doubt God calls his children to make exertions beyond their strength, and to sacrifice health and life in His cause, but certainly not as a general thing. If we do nothing from our own native impulses, but simply obey the Inward Voice, we shall generally find our bodily strength equal to the task imposed. When we lay out our own work and are determined to drive through with it at all hazards, and go forward in our own will and way, the work may be good, but we have left our Guide, and shall be very likely to transgress some physical law. It appears to me that in most of the cases where health has been lost through over exertion, it was in this manner. "Godliness is profitable unto all things, having promise of the life that now is, and of that which is to come."

Within a few years there has been in this country a great reform in regard to *drinking*, and it has operated most happily on the interests of religion.

Another reform is now called for; and that is in the matter of *eating*. Many articles of food are in constant use which it is well known are unfavorable to health. Our Heavenly Father has provided us with a great variety of food which is simple and wholesome, why then should we accustom ourselves to the use of that which is neither?

Many considerations of health, convenience, economy, intellectual vigor, and high-toned spirituality might be brought forward in favor of simple food, and nothing can be said against it. Yet every day, throughout Christendom, these considerations are all set aside merely for the gratification of an artificial appetite. The inspired Apostle if he were here now would say to us, "For this cause many are weak and sickly among you, and many sleep."

There certainly must be a reform in this particular before the Church will become deeply spiritual. The command is, "Loose thyself from the bands of thy neck, O captive daughter of Zion." One of these bands is the indulgence of appetite, and it must be loosed, before she will "put on strength."

All Christians who make high attainments in the Divine life seem, at some period in their course, to have had their minds exercised on this point. Many have tried to think it was too small a matter to be treated religiously, but the Spirit withstood them, and they were compelled to yield.

The author of the "Interior Life" remarks, in a valuable chapter on this subject, "The life of God in the soul has a much closer connection with modes of living than is generally supposed. If Christians, instead of indulging and pampering the appetite for meats and drinks, would be satisfied with simple nourishment, and with that small quantity which is adequate to all the purposes of nature, what abundant blessings would infallibly result both to body and mind! Many dark hours, which are now the subject of sad complaints on the part of professed Christians, would be exchanged for bright ones. God would then reveal his face of affectionate love, which it is impossible for Him to do to those who enslave themselves in this manner."

Devout Christians in all ages have found fasting highly beneficial. If occasional abstinence is salutary, as giving the spiritual part of our nature an ascendancy for the time over the corporeal part, is not habitual temperance, both in regard to the quantity and quality of our food, still better? Is there not a palpable inconsistency in occasionally fasting, and habitually feasting?

Here as in the matter of dress it is not easy to lay down rules—we can only lay down principles. But let us not forget the Scripture rule, "Whether therefore ye eat and drink, or whatsoever ye do, do all to the glory of God." Does not this forbid the habitual use of rich and unwholesome food, as well as stimulating and intoxicating drinks?

It is commonly remarked that we find the most striking instances of piety amongst the poor. Perhaps one reason of this is, that they do not dim their spiritual perception by the indulgence of appetite. I believe Christians have always found that if they would be holy, they must be abstemious. When we surrender all to God, our appetites are among the things which are laid on the altar. Thenceforth they are to be regarded only with reference to the objects for which they were implanted, and never to be indulged simply or chiefly to please ourselves. True piety is eminently favorable to health. In the millennium I expect people will have perfect health, because all will obey the laws of their physical nature; and several generations having been thus obedient, there will probably be no hereditary tendencies to disease.

It appears to me that a Christian female placed in the providence of God at the head of a family, if she would be consistent, should not only be abstemious herself, but avoid furnishing for her household such articles of food as she knows to be injurious. Females should be enlightened on this subject, as it lies with them to bring about a reform.

The command of the Saviour is, "Take no thought, saying, what shall we eat? or what shall we drink?" Now, studying cookery books and toiling over cakes and pastry, looks very much like a violation of this precept. I know that some plausible excuses may be offered for a compliance with custom in this respect; but whether they would all amount to a good and sufficient *reason*, is a question for each one to settle.

May you, my dear Eugenia, always have wisdom to decide what is right, and courage to act up to your decisions! Yours affectionately.

LETTER XVII.

THE DISCIPLINE OF LIFE.

Dear Eugenia,—We have been now a long time considering the *Duties* of life, let us turn our thoughts for a moment to its *Discipline.*

At your age it is natural to look on the sunny side, and to fancy that you shall find a smoother path than those who have gone before you. While I am far from desiring you to take gloomy views of life, or to afflict yourself with anticipations of evil, I would wish you to look at things as they are, and to regard this probationary state in the true, rational, and scriptural light. You are happy now, and everything to your young imagination is bright and promising; but it will not be always so; nor should you wish it.

God never designed this world for our home; *it is only the place where we are to be educated for eternity.* His words to us are, "Arise and depart, for this is not your rest." But we are bent on making a rest of it, and eagerly gather around us all the comforts within reach, in order that it may be as home-like and pleasant as possible. This disposition of ours obliges the Lord to speak to us by his providences, repeating in a tone not to be misunderstood, "Arise and depart, for this is not your rest."

At first we look up in surprise, when our treasures are taken away, or our plans are overturned, as if some strange thing had happened to us. But the sooner we give up the idea of looking upon this world as a place of enjoyment the better. We shall never be able to regard the circumstances and events of life in their true light till we do. I am surprised to observe that even those who indulge the hope that they are Christians often reach middle life before they learn to see things in the light of the Bible. You can perceive from the manner in which most people talk, that they regard enjoyment as the great object of pursuit. But the Bible represents life as a race, in which we are to run for a prize—as a battle-field, where many foes are to be encountered—as a place where we are to be trained for another state of existence.

I often compare this life to a *Boarding School.*

You remember your feelings when you were sent away from home to attend a distant academy. It was painful to be for so long a time absent from your father's house; but you submitted cheerfully to this, and many other privations, because you knew it was to fit you for subsequent usefulness. You had some hard lessons to learn, and some disagreeable regulations to submit to. Then your boarding house was not much like the pleasant home you had left. But you made the best of it, knowing that nothing else was to be expected at school; and the idea of being thus fitted to take your place in society, and act well your part, was ever before you. You did not fret at the difficult tasks imposed by the teachers; you were willing to study hard, and submit to all the restraints and regulations of the school, and to all the inconveniences of your temporary home, for it was a matter of course. But how glad you were when the time drew near to return to your father's house! How joyfully you packed up your books and clothes, and prepared for the journey! Perhaps you shed some tears at parting with your schoolmates, but the thought of home—sweet home—soon dried them! You returned to your father's house, and took the place you were then prepared to fill in the family circle, with a glad heart, and with no regrets on account of the hard lessons and salutary discipline of school.

Such it seems to me is the true light in which to

regard this life. We are here learning those lessons, and receiving that discipline, which is to fit us for another state. This is not our life; it is only the preface—the introduction. The grand arena of our enjoyments and achievements is in the spirit world. Our Father would have us live constantly with reference to that, gratefully receive his lessons and his discipline—entering into his designs and co-operating with him. When our education here is finished, let us joyfully accept the permission to *go home*. In our Father's house of many mansions we shall then find ourselves fitted to take a place.

You often hear disappointed people say this is a poor world. It is so because they don't take it right. As a place of enjoyment it is a poor world; but it is a good school—a good place to work for God—a good place in which to glorify him by cheerful suffering—a good place in which to fit for heaven; and this is all He ever meant it should be—at least till men become holy—then no doubt it will present quite another aspect.

Our Father says that we must through much tribulation enter into the Kingdom of Heaven. Why? Not because he loves to trouble us? By no means; this is not an arbitrary arrangement of his—it grows out of the nature of the case. Sin necessarily involves suffering. Suffering has in itself a salutary tendency, and when sanctified seems to do that for the soul which nothing else will. At least this is generally the case; though we know that the Holy Spirit can work if he pleases without such instrumentality.

You desire to be holy—to be perfect and entire wanting nothing. While endeavoring, as I trust you are, to follow out the principles laid down in these letters, you will no doubt be daily praying that God would "sanctify you wholly," and that "your whole spirit and soul and body be preserved blameless." At the same time you will I hope throw yourself in full, affectionate confidence on the promise; "Faithful is He that calleth you, who also will do it." How will He do it? Partly in all probability through suffering.

Perhaps you will remind me that the Saviour's prayer was, "Sanctify them through thy truth." Yes, it is through the truth that we are to be sanctified; that is, by understanding, believing, loving and obeying it. Now affliction is a great quickener to the mind in all these exercises. The general testimony of devout Christians is to this effect: "I never fully understood such and such things in the Bible till I was afflicted, and they met my case; I never before so heartily believed them; never before were they so precious to me; never before was I so impressed with the importance of entire obedience." Accept of afflictions, then, with thanksgiving, as an answer to your prayers for sanctification, and endeavor to derive from them the greatest possible benefit.

My dear Eugenia, I am very desirous that you should take just and scriptural views of life. The world calculate on getting all the enjoyment here they possibly can, but this should not be your aim. You can afford to wait for your good things. I do not mean to say there is nothing here to enjoy; there is a great deal! but it is not to be sought as *the principal thing;* it is not to be made too much of; it is not to be separated from God. When He sends sunshine, rejoice in it *as his gift*, and when He darkens your sky, and sends storms, accept them with thanksgiving; for the last is as great a proof of his love as the first, and therefore as much a cause for gratitude.

With this view of things you see there are a number of words in common use for which you will have no occasion; such as *disappointment*, *regret*, *fear*, and *anxiety*. If you believe that God orders all things, and love to have it so, there will be no occasion to make use of those common expressions—"I am afraid this or that will happen;" "I am sorry it is so;" "I wish;" "unfortunately," &c. The use of such expressions seems inconsistent with obedience to the command, "Rejoice evermore," and incompatible with the idea of entire satisfaction with the Divine government.

What is the meaning of the word *blessing?* A friend of mine defines it, "*That which comes from God.*" An excellent definition. If you accept it, you will perceive that life is an unbroken series of *blessings.* Some are sweet, and others are bitter—the one is food for the soul, the other medicine. Now the bitter blessings are even a greater mark of God's love to us than the sweet, because it pains him to send them, and because they generally do us the most good. Therefore if we take the right view, and cherish right feelings, it will be easy to thank God, *on the instant,* for every painful thing that comes to us. Indeed, if we are truly consecrated to Him, the continual prayer of our hearts is, "Thy will be done," and the continual joy of our hearts will be, that it *is* done. Yes, irrespective of its bearing on our spiritual interests, we shall have a constant holy joy in the thought that the Lord reigns, and that His glorious plan is daily unfolding.

If you enter on the joys, sorrows, cares, and responsibilities of life with these high views and feelings, you cannot fail to be a happy and useful Christian.

Ever yours.

" What matter whether pain or pleasures fill
  The swelling heart one little moment here ?
From both alike how vain is every thrill,
  While an untried eternity is near !
Think not of rest, fond man, in life's career ;
  The joys and grief that meet thee, dash aside
Like bubbles, and thy bark right onward steer
  Through calm and tempest, till it cross the tide,
Shoot into port in triumph, or serenely glide."

LETTER XVIII.

SERIES CONCLUDED.

Dear Eugenia,—It is time to bring these letters to a close; but before doing so, let us briefly review the ground we have gone over.

In the first place, we considered the nature of *Entire Consecration to God*, and found that it implied more than young Christians are generally able to comprehend. But if they lay all on the altar, *as far as they can see*, they are accepted. If they continue to be thus fully given up, their eyes will be opened to see the secret workings of selfishness, they will be led to renounce them as fast as discerned, and as fast as they discover and renounce any form of inordinate self-love (which is the root of all sin), it is their privilege to believe that they are *accepted*, and reckon themselves dead to it, through our Lord Jesus Christ; that is, calculating that they have nothing more to do with it, confidently relying on His promise of keeping them.

2. You have seen that the only way to advance, or even to hold on to what has been gained, is *by venturing to appropriate those exceeding great and precious promises*, which the inspired apostle says will make you a partaker of the Divine nature, and

enable you to escape the corruption that is in the world. You are to cherish an unwavering confidence that in every temptation God will make a way of escape; that he will write his law in your heart; that he will preserve you blameless, and sanctify you wholly. Especially are you to avail yourself of the crowning promise of all, that the Holy Spirit shall come and take up his abode in your heart, to regulate and control every feeling and motive, to comfort, bring to remembrance, hold you back from sin, and guide you into truth and duty. All this He offers to do *if you will permit Him.*

3. You have seen also that there is an important work to be done in the *crucifixion of the desires;* viz., the appetites, propensities, and affections. These are not to be extinguished, but regulated and brought under control, being made subservient to the ends for which they were given, and used only for the glory of God. This crucifixion of the desires is not so well understood by Christians generally as it ought to be. You must make it a subject of specific attention, if you would be sanctified wholly.

4. We have seen the importance of taking the *Bible* as the only standard of faith and practice. I trust you have resolved, whatever others may do, you will be *a Bible Christian*—that you will do what the Bible requires, avoid what the Bible forbids, and accept all the Bible promises.

5. We have looked at *Prayer*, and found it to be the sweet privilege of communion with our Father. Petitions should be largely intermingled with praises, and with expressions of affectionate confidence that He can do the thing that we ask, and will, if it is best.

6. We have considered the Divine law in regard to the *choice of Associates*, and especially in *Choosing a Companion for life*. The great rule here is, to marry only *in the Lord*, and this in fact is the great rule for doing everything.

7. The importance of ordering our *Conversation* aright has also been considered. We must not waste our Master's time in idle chit-chat, nor pervert the noble gift of speech to any unworthy purpose, but regard it ever as a most important talent to be used for Him.

8. Our *Reading*, too, we have seen, must be only that which the Spirit directs. We are not at liberty to read for amusement, or even to gratify a thirst for knowledge, any farther than He permits.

9. All our *Occupations* must be chosen with reference to the Divine approbation; and we are to be careful that they do not take the form of *busy idleness*.

10. *Social Duties* must be faithfully discharged; including those which grow out of our relations to the family, the church, and the community.

11. In regard to *Dress*, the rule laid down was, not to go beyond the requirements of comfort and propriety; and not to allow ourselves in any indulgence which might cause a weak believer to offend, or be offended.

12. *A due observance of the laws of our physical nature* we have seen to be important in its bearings on health, and consequently on comfort and usefulness. The Scripture rule is, "Whether therefore ye eat or drink, or whatsoever ye do, do all to the glory of God."

Finally, after taking this survey of the *duties* of life, we considered its *Discipline.*

"Not enjoyment and not sorrow
 Is our destined end or way—
But to live that each to-morrow
 Find us further than to-day."

Everything is to be received with thanksgiving, for all is sent in love—the bitter no less than the sweet. We are to look on this life only as the preparatory stage of our existence, where we are to be educated for eternity.

May you, my dear Eugenia, be inclined to profit by these hints! Do not say the standard is placed too high. Certainly it is not higher than the Bible; nor is it anything more than is implied in that act of surrender with which every Christian sets out in the Divine life. All these things are involved in your church covenant. This is not merely a beautiful theory, it is what many by the grace of God have attained. I know the mass of Christians now do not reach it, but the fact that some do settles the question of its practicability. The same grace which carried them to these happy heights is freely offered to you.

Does not your heart burn with desire to be all that it is your privilege to be? all that God would have you to be? Does it not look to you infinitely desirable to be holy? "Blessed are they that hunger and thirst after righteousness, for they shall be filled." The provisions of the Gospel are sufficient to meet every want of the soul. The Saviour says, "If thou canst believe—all things are possible to him that believeth." The Psalmist says, "He shall preserve thee from *all* evil." The Apostle says, "My God will supply all your need." Only put Him to the test, and see how great things He will do for you.

Be not disheartened because so few find a present and full salvation. When one of the disciples said, "Lord, are there few that be saved?" His answer was, "Strive to enter in at the strait gate." The way of holiness is a narrow way, and few there be that find it. Do you ask what is meant by this *striving?* It consists in a continual self-renunciation, and a continual effort to shake off old habits of unbelief. You have probably not been accustomed to believe that God would do all for *you* which he offers to do for the Church. So long as this unbelief continues, you make it impossible for Him to fulfil to you his great and precious promises. O how many souls there are like the city of Nazareth, where He "can do no mighty work, because of their unbelief!"

The Apostle says, "Let us labor to enter into this rest." What rest? *The rest of faith.* "We that believe," he adds, "*do* enter into rest." How would he have us *labor* to enter in? The labor consists in renouncing self, and breaking up the old habits of unbelief. There is a great deal o. striving and laboring among conscientious Christians which has in it much of legality They have followed after holiness, but have not attained it. Wherefore? Because they sought it not by faith, but as it were by the works of the law. They have been trying to make themselves better, and they wonder at their small success. If, instead of this, they would give themselves fully to God, and renounce their unbelief, then he would do that for them which they now try in vain to do for themselves.

Dear Eugenia, I speak from experience—having tried both ways. For years I adopted the system of rules and resolutions, and made little or no progress. Then I saw the promise *afar off*; but since I have embraced them, they have been constantly fulfilled to me. Thus will you find it. "Venture on them—venture wholly." The Lord is now saying, "Be it unto you according to your faith." If you believe for little, you shall have little—believe for much, and you shall have much—believe for all, and you shall have all.

In the bonds of Christian love, ever yours.

"Awake, my soul! stretch every nerve,
And press with vigor on;
A heavenly race demands thy zeal,
A bright, immortal crown.

'Tis God's all-animating voice
That calls thee from on high;
'Tis his own hand presents the prize
To thine aspiring eye.

A cloud of witnesses around
Hold thee in full survey;
Forget the steps already trod,
And ONWARD urge thy way.

Blest Saviour! introduced by thee,
Our race have we begun;
And, crowned with victory, at thy feet
We'll lay our laurels down."

www.ingramcontent.com/pod-product-compliance
Lightning Source LLC
LaVergne TN
LVHW021427110826
845150LV00007B/2119

9781425507527